A THIRD OF US

ENDORSEMENTS

Recently I came across an (older) article dismissing the terminology of the "Unreached" for a lack of clarity. Dr. Marv Newell's book provides just that: clarity to the nature of the unreached, clarity of our Savior's commission, and clarity of the gospel message that we live and proclaim. It is a pleasure to commend to you Dr. Newell's book, *A Third of Us: What It Takes to Reach the Unreached*, as a gospel-centered theology of mission for today's world.

STEVE COFFEY, DSL | executive director, Christar USA

The cause of the unreached has been lost in the business of the church. This book is a rally cry for all Christians. Dr. Newell makes a strong and clear case that will light a fire in the hearts of believers.

JON FUGLER | board chairperson, Alliance for the Unreached

It is a sobering thought to those of us in the mission community that two thousand years after receiving our marching orders from Jesus, with the Great Commission, more than a third of the world's population is still unreached. Marv's words are a must-read for individuals, churches, and agencies alike to bring focus and initiative to reach those destined for an eternity separated from God.

SCOTT HOLBROOK | president, Avant Ministries

The Great Commission to make disciples of all nations, over two thousand years ago, remains unfinished today! Dr. Newell's book points out how Jesus' chronological commissions continue to be relevant for finishing the task of world evangelization. An essential resource for every church leader, local pastor, and seminary professor.

KEN KATAYAMA | CEO and president, Crossover Global

If you are passionate about the final words of Jesus, then you must read this book! Marv does an amazing job of describing the Great Commission and the imperative nature of every believer to find their expression of involvement. He will give you scriptural support, statistics, and inspiring testimonies. This book will open your eyes fresh and anew to the realities of those who still wait for their first encounter with Jesus.

GREG KELLEY | CEO and executive director, World Mission

God has always had the redemption of individuals on his heart! Getting the good news to every man, woman, and child on planet earth is on his mind and heart. As believers, we have a unique privilege of seeing the reality of people's coming into God's eternal family. Psalm 2:8 is a template for us: "Ask of Me, and I will make the nations your inheritance and the ends of the earth your possession." As a believer, as I ask God for the nations, he will respond with opportunities for expansion of his kingdom. Marv Newell gives a compelling case for each of our involvement in reaching people. Read and have your spiritual imagination enlarged.

LAUREN LIBBY | international president, TWR International

There is no book more important during these significant global challenges and gospel opportunities. As someone who has dedicated his life to reaching the unreached, I'm so excited and challenged by this significant work from Marv Newell to get into the hands and hearts of God's people. May God use this book to see a new wave of gospel servants dedicate their lives to "bring the gospel to the last third of peoples globally"! May we commit together to pray and put into practice these challenging truths from my good friend and global colleague.

DAVE MEYERS | CEO, ZimZam Global

We pay close attention to a person's "last words" before they leave this life. Jesus' last words were his command to make disciples of *every* ethnic group to the very ends of the earth. We should pay attention. One third of the world population is "unreached," with no access to the gospel. Yet only 1 percent of mission giving goes to reach the unreached. And only 3 percent of the missionary workforce works among the unreached one-third. Marv Newell points to the urgency of our Lord's mandate and outlines the methods and means to reach over three billion people with no church, no Bible, no missionary. Marv's writing is well-researched, compelling, and convicting. Reading and digesting this important book will change your perspective and could change your life. Highly recommended reading!

WAYNE PEDERSON | global ambassador, Far East Broadcasting (FEBC)

A THIRD OF US

What It Takes to Reach the Unreached

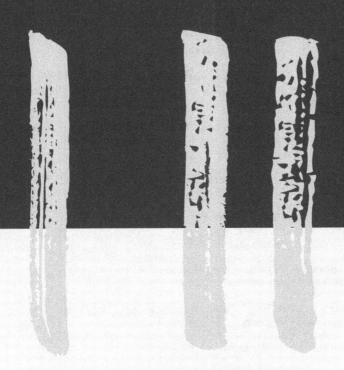

Marvin J. Newell

Portions of this book previously appeared under the title *Commissioned What Jesus Wants You To Know As You Go* by Marvin J. Newell, ChurchSmart Resources, St. Charles, IL.

Published by William Carey Publishing
10 W. Dry Creek Cir
Littleton, CO 80120 | www.missionbooks.org

William Carey Publishing is a ministry of Frontier Ventures
Pasadena, CA 91104 | www.frontierventures.org

Cover Designers: Will Echols, Branches Mission Lab, and Mike Riester
Interior Designer: Mike Riester
Copyeditor: Andy Sloan
Managing Editor: Melissa Hicks

ISBNs: 978-1-64508-403-7 (paperback)
       978-1-64508-406-8 (epub)

Printed Worldwide

25 24 23 22 21   1 2 3 4 5   IN

Library of Congress Control Number: 2021944018

DEDICATION

This book is dedicated to
every frontline missionary
living among unreached
peoples all over the world,
sharing the good news of
Jesus with those who have
never heard. Your dedication
to this high yet difficult
calling makes you worthy
of this book's dedication.

CONTENTS

PREFACE

We talk about the Second Coming;
half the world has not heard of the first.

—Oswald J. Smith

I did not write this book to put readers on a guilt trip for complacency in mission involvement. Other well-intentioned mission authors have already done that to one degree or another. Rather, the focus of this book is to bring a well-defined awareness to believers of the vastness of the task that remains if all peoples are to have the opportunity to hear the gospel of Jesus Christ.

We live in an age that values and strives for fairness, justice, and equality—and rightfully so. These are core biblical values. Ideally, when these standards are broadly applied, they bring physical and social wholesomeness and well-being to humans, no matter who they may be. And that is a very good thing.

But few have stopped to consider the responsibility of exerting the same effort for the spiritual well-being of mankind, the chief gospel value. How fair is it that three billion people have yet to hear the name of Jesus in a meaningful way?[1] How just is it that a third of the world's population is denied access to the gospel? How equal is it that gospel-enriched areas of the globe hoard spiritual resources, while vast swaths of humanity live in spiritual deprivation and gospel ignorance? Yet there is a general unawareness among believers of these realities. And that is a very bad thing.

These conditions demand our attention. Thus, we turn to the words of Jesus to obtain insight into how we, who know and believe the gospel, can bring spiritual fairness, justice, and equality to the world. We do this by giving the opportunity to everyone, everywhere a chance to hear the gospel of Jesus Christ. By taking a fresh look at the five "Great Commission" passages that he left us, the substance, scope, and strategy for reaching the unreached becomes remarkably clear.

Why does this book take a deep dive into these final commands of our resurrected Lord? Because through these passages Jesus conveys details of our responsibility of spreading the story of redemption to the nations. They contain the guiding principles for reaching the world today.

A past mission writer, Herbert Kane, rightly observed, "There are many reasons why the church should engage in world evangelization,

---

1 According to Joshua Project (https://joshuaproject.net), a more exact amount is that 42 percent of the world is considered unreached. For didactic and communication purposes, the Alliance for the Unreached has chosen to use the count and the mark/symbol for *A Third of Us*–a third of humanity–which is slightly under the reality but drives the point home.

but the paramount reason is the command of Christ."[2] John Stott added, "We engage in evangelism today not because we want to, or because we choose to or because we like to, but because we have been told to. The Church is under orders. The risen Lord has commanded us to 'go' to 'preach,' to 'make disciples' and that is enough for us."[3]

The central premise of this book is that when it comes to sharing the gospel, no ethnic group is to be excluded. None are to be ignored. No group is to be considered too far away, too remote, too small, too insignificant, or too unworthy of our efforts. The life-changing message of repentance and forgiveness of sins in Jesus is to be offered to all.

It is my hope that this book will bring awareness of the spiritual plight of the third of humanity who have no access to the gospel. Further, I hope that with that awareness will come an understanding of what it takes to reach these unreached. Lastly, I hope that with that understanding will come a greater mobilization of prayer, people, and resources for the cause of reaching A Third of Us. May you be so inspired.

—Marvin J. Newell
August 2021

---

2 J. Herbert Kane, *Christian Missions in Biblical Perspective* (Baker, 1976), 43–44.
3 John Stott, "The Great Commission," in *One Race, One Gospel, One Task*, Vol. 1, edited by Carl F. H. Henry and W. S. Mooneyham (World Wide Publications, 1967), 37.

CHAPTER 1

Who Are "A Third of Us"?

"A third of anything is significant."

—Marvin J. Newell

Forty-two-year-old Mrs. Taufik is the mother of two teenagers, and one wife of her husband's two. He splits his time between his younger wife in the coastal city of Padang, on the west coast of Sumatra, Indonesia, but less and less time with her in the mountainous interior town of Bukittinggi ("High Mountain").

As an ethnic Minangkabau, Mrs. Taufik is a staunch Muslim, along with 99.72 percent of her people. The Minangkabau people have a saying: "To be Minangkabau is to be Muslim." Scanning every direction from her home she can see dozens of mosques that, at 5:00 a.m. every morning, vie for her attention with loud calls from their minarets by piercing the dawn, declaring that God is Great. That masculine blare gets her up each morning for the first of five prayers that she will offer to Allah throughout the day.

Life is rather monotonous for Mrs. Taufik, but with her husband seldom present she wraps her life around the needs of her growing children. Thankfully, her husband sends her enough rupiah each month (although he often misses a month) to meet her minimal needs, though she can barely squeak by. To make up for the lack, she harvests the kangkong (spinach-like plants) that grows in abundance in the ditch running behind her small house. She cuts some each morning and takes it to the market to sell at her twelve-feet by twelve-feet wooden stall. With the meager profit, she purchases fresh foods at the market before heading home at noon.

As an unreached person, Mrs. Taufik has no opportunity to access three life-giving essentials so common to us who know Jesus as Savior and Lord.

After the village-wide two-hour siesta, she spends the rest of the afternoon caring for her two daughters, and then makes certain that the three of them are at the mosque by seven o'clock for final prayers. Once home, she goes to bed, only to start the same routine the following day. Only Friday, the day of corporate worship at the mosque, is different.

As an unreached person, Mrs. Taufik has no opportunity to access three life-giving essentials so common to us who know Jesus as Savior and Lord. Although portions of the Bible have been translated into her language, she is not aware of that, and there is no one in the vicinity to tell her. She lives in an area where there are no churches—all she sees around her are myriads of mosques. Finally, there are no Jesus-followers for her to meet, even if she had reason to do so.

Mrs. Taufik lives in what those in mission circles call an unreached "frontier people group"—living out her existence on the frontier beyond gospel awareness, together with the estimated 6,815,000 other members of her "people group."

The Unfinished Task

Ever since the Day of Pentecost, devoted followers of Christ have avidly taken the good news of Jesus across continents, countries, and cultures. Yet after two thousand years, the reaching of all peoples, like the Minangkabau of Sumatra, with this good news is still incomplete. This is true even though no other effort in the history of humankind compares in scope and expenditure to this undertaking. Literally hundreds of thousands of message-bearers have been sent, billions of dollars have been expended, and innumerable prayers have been offered on behalf of the quest to give every human being an opportunity to hear the gospel.

Over the centuries, dozens of vibrant regional sending centers have sent out message-bearers, and they continue to do so. Although the propagation of the gospel has continued unbroken and unabated for centuries, the task remains unfinished.

Today, a third of humanity—A Third of Us—do not have access to the gospel! Stop a moment to think about that. *More than three billion people have yet to hear the good news of Jesus,* having no opportunity to believe in him as Savior from their sins and to make peace with God. Of all the injustices in the world—and there are many that are quite distressing—this is the most serious of all. Why is that? *Because of the eternal consequences for that one third who have no opportunity to hear the good news of Jesus Christ.* A third of anything is significant, especially this third.

This is not to say that believers have ignored the spiritual plight of the lost. Throughout history, message-bearers have been sent to many places and peoples to proclaim the good news. Some have had remarkable and distinguished ministries. Others, comprising the vast majority of those who have gone out, have served quietly and inconspicuously. Most have given up much, through self-denial, only to see little response. Nevertheless, this much can be said of all: They served in the past and are serving in the present in obedience to the call of God on their lives to reach the unreached.

Even with all these efforts, the task remains unfinished for the third who have yet to be exposed to the good news of salvation. So who and where is this remaining third of us?

The Three "Nos"

Although remarkable progress has been made on some fronts, the fact remains that a third of humanity has no contact with the gospel and remains unreached. What exactly is meant by this term unreached? Put simply, the term refers to large swaths of humanity who have no access to the gospel. Unreached people have little or no significant contact with three life-giving essentials that are common to followers of Christ. These essentials can be summed up as "the three nos": no Bible,[4] no church, and no known believers.[5]

The designation, or description, of these three nos is not new. Frank Severn, the former executive director of SEND International, mentioned them in an article he wrote in 1997 when he stated, "It would be good if every church would focus some of its mission resources on a people group 'which has no church, no Bible, and no believers.'"[6] More recently, Rick Warren, in the context of the Finishing the Task movement, has popularized "the three nos" correspondingly as "the three Bs." He frequently refers to unreached people groups as having "No Believers, No Bible, and No Body of Christ."[7]

---

4 Thanks to the untiring efforts of Bible translators over recent years, portions of the Bible, if not the entire Bible, have been translated into many of the languages of these unreached groups. But the awareness and distribution of these Scriptures is woefully wanting. The majority of people within these groups don't know that a Bible translation exists; or if they do know, they don't care.

5 Some people groups have such a minuscule number of believers that it is as if there were none at all. The category of "no known believers" technically refers to people groups in which less than 2 percent of the population are believers, but in most cases it is even less. Most of these people groups have zero believers. A close approximation of "no known believers" are "frontier people groups" on Joshua Project lists: https://joshuaproject.net/frontier.

6 Frank Severn, "Some Thoughts on the Meaning of All Nations," *Evangelical Missions Quarterly* 33, no. 4 (1997).

7 See the Finishing the Task website: finishingthetask.com.

Let's take a moment to consider these three nos. Imagine living in an area where there are no believers in Jesus. With no Christ-followers in the vicinity, the residents would have no opportunity to encounter the gospel through another person who could personally explain it. A friendly face and a sympathetic heart would be absent to cordially convey the saving power of the gospel. "Salt" and "light" within the community would be nonexistent. It would be a spiritually dark place—a place of lostness, with no hope and with no one to show the way.

Secondly, imagine having no access to the Bible. Without the availability of Scripture, God's written revelation intended for all of humankind would not be obtainable. God's prescribed way for living would be absent. God's moral standards would be ignorantly violated. God's message of hope would not be known. God's requirement of belief and repentance could not be read. Worst of all, the story of the Savior Jesus could not be understood and appreciated.

Lastly, imagine if there were no church. This doesn't necessarily refer to a church building, but more importantly to a body of Christ-followers who display communion with Jesus and each other. Without a community of Christ-followers, there would be no gathering together with others of like precious faith for encouragement. There would be no fellowship with like-minded believers, bringing health to the soul and strength to godly commitment. For lack of social interaction, there would be no possibility of being built up in the faith. There would be no disciple-making. This would be a place of lonely, spiritual barrenness. There would be no ability to start and sustain a movement for Christ.

These three together is what is meant by having no access to the gospel. No believers. No Bible. No church. And this is indeed the current plight of over a third of humanity—*A Third of Us.*

Where Are the Nos?

Naturally the question arises, "Just where are these Nos found?" The answer can be a bit complex, but not difficult. The unreached are found in three broad arenas.

Imbedded in Unreached People Groups

Those of us who live in modern globalized, urbanized, and high-tech nations often miss or ignore the fact that smaller "nations," known as people groups, exist within larger nations. These ethno-linguistic clusters are distinguished by their distinct language, culture, and worldview; and they typically inhabit ancestral lands that have been theirs for generations.

Mrs. Taufik, as a Minangkabau living in southwest Sumatra, is a prime example. Although she is Indonesian by nationality, she prefers to identify herself by her tribal heritage. Being Minangkabau is the identity that is most dear to her.

Ever since the 1974 Lausanne Congress on World Evangelization, varying definitions for "people groups," and with it, "unreached people groups," have been offered. Each successive attempt has endeavored to improve and clarify. They come into play as we consider reaching A Third of Us.

One of the more recent and probably best definitions of unreached peoples comes from David Platt, a deeply committed mission-minded pastor and past president of the International Mission Board of the Southern Baptist Convention, one of the largest missions in North America. He states,

> Unreached peoples and places are those among whom Christ is largely unknown and the church is relatively insufficient to make Christ known in its broader population without outside help.[8]

The three Nos align with this definition.

But one may wonder how many ethno-linguistic people groups there are, and how many of them comprise the unreached third of us. According to research-oriented Joshua Project,[9] the world contains 17,468 distinct people groups. Of these, 7,419 (or 41.8 percent) are classified as unreached.[10] These unreached people groups contain 3.2 billion of the 7.8 billion people in the world today—well over A Third of Us!

The following table displays a clear way to understand the current status of people groups. Viewed graphically, the world's population can be divided into three distinct categories using the "full access, some access, no access" paradigm."[11]

---

8 David Platt, "Rethinking Unreached Peoples," Desiring God website, February 13, 2019, https://www.desiringgod.org/articles/rethinking-unreached-peoples.
9 Joshua Project is a directing member of the Alliance for the Unreached.
10 https://joshuaproject.net.
11 David Barrett defines these categories as follows: World C: all persons who individually are Christians anywhere in the world. This is Christianity in its broadest expression and includes Roman Catholic, Orthodox, Protestant, Anglican, evangelical, and all derived or deviant forms of Christianity. World B: all non-Christians who have heard the gospel or who live within societies and areas where they were or are likely to hear it during their lifetime. These are evangelized non-Christians. World A: all non-Christians who are unevangelized and likely to remain so without a new effort by Christians to take the gospel to them. Referenced by Patrick Johnstone in The Church Is Bigger Than You Think, 67–68.

World Population: 7.8 Billion

UNREACHED & UNSAVED No witnessing community within their people group or area. 3.2 billion / 41 percent	**No Access**
UNDER-REACHED & UNSAVED Most have never had a clear presentation of the gospel, although it is nearby. 2.14 billion / 28 percent	**Some Access**
REACHED BUT NOT SAVED Some knowledge of the gospel, nominal acceptance, "Traditional Christians" in name only. 1.56 billion / 20 percent — *and* — **REACHED & SAVED** True followers of Christ. 900 million / 11 percent	**Full Access**

As Christ-followers, besides being concerned for those with no access who comprise the top tier of this graphic (our main focus), we also need to understand what it means to be one of those who have full access to the gospel and are considered "Reached and Saved" (or to use a biblical euphemism, "born again"). To make sure we have it correct, a true follower of Christ is one who believes:

1. *The Bible to be God's unique revelation to man—truthful and trustworthy in all that it says, from start to finish.*
2. *Jesus to be the unique incarnation of God—fully God and fully man. Jesus, the Jewish Messiah, lived a sinless and perfect life on earth, thus qualifying him to become the Redeemer of mankind.*
3. *Salvation is only through the redemptive work of Jesus Christ when he died an atoning death on the cross for humankind—something a person must personally believe and accept by faith in this life.*
4. *He or she is responsible to witness to the lost, as a means of bringing them to faith in Christ.* [12]

---

12 I am indebted to Patrick Johnstone for presenting these in broad categories in his book *The Church Is Bigger Than You Think.*

As seen in the previous table, 89 percent of the world's population are not true followers of Jesus. But more alarmingly, and this is our main concern, 42 percent don't even have a chance to become true followers of Jesus because they have such limited access to the gospel.

So this people group reality, coupled with the "access" perspective, is one way of seeing where A Third of Us are located.

Besides being imbedded in unreached people groups, there is a second arena in which those without any access to the gospel are found.

Insulated in Other Religions

Not only are A Third of Us found imbedded in unreached people groups, they are also insulated or encased in other belief systems. These billions of people are so protectively enclosed within their traditional religions that it is difficult for the gospel to gain access. Now don't think that these non-Christian peoples don't believe in something, for mankind is innately religious. But their religious traditions have built walls of protection around them so that their religious traditions and way of life insulate them from disruption and change—the very things that occur when people are exposed to the gospel.

Statistically, this is how the number of adherents of the world's major religions can currently be understood:[13]

Size of Major Religious Groups, 2020	
Religion	Percent
Christianity	31.4%
Islam	23.2%
Hinduism	15.4%
Unaffiliated	14.1%
Buddhism	7.1%
Folk Religion	5.9%
Other (includes Judaism, Bahá'í, Sikhism, and Jainism)	1.0%
Pew Research Center, 2015	

---

13 https://www.pewforum.org/2015/04/02/religious-projections-2010-2050/. Note that the survey done by Pew in 2015 projected the data for 2020.

One may ask, "Isn't it a good thing that most people belong to a religion? After all, can't God work through other religions to bring people to himself?" That is a delicate question that needs to be addressed—for why bother with reaching unreached peoples if

> **Although there may be points of similarity between Christianity and some other religions, there are clear, fundamental differences that make them incongruent.**

somehow, in some way, through some other belief or means, people can be saved? If this is so, let's leave Mrs. Taufik alone, because her sincere belief in the teachings of the Qur'an is enough to have God accept her, right?

Although there may be points of similarity between Christianity and some other religions, there are clear, fundamental differences that make them incongruent. I recall a noted Christian apologist once saying that the popular aphorism, "All religions are fundamentally the same and only superficially different," simply is not true. It is more correct to say that all religions are superficially similar but fundamentally different.

This especially holds true when it comes to belief in the gospel. God tells us that our root issue and spiritual predicament is sin (Rom 3:23). All people are sinners by nature and by choice; and only belief in Jesus, the sinless Son of God, who paid the penalty for that sin when he died on the cross, can bring forgiveness for those sins.

One disconcerting fact about gospel access when it comes to considering adherents of other religions is that very few Buddhists, Hindus, or Muslims personally know a Christian from whom they can encounter the gospel. Formal research bears this out. Mission researcher Todd Johnson states,

> *Broadly speaking, Buddhists, Hindus and Muslims have relatively little contact with Christians, and this has not changed much in the last two decades. An estimated 87 percent of Buddhists, Hindus and Muslims do not personally know a Christian.*[14]

Probably the opposite is true too: 87 percent of Christians do not personally know a Buddhist, Hindu, or Muslim. With this lack of personal

---

14 Todd M. Johnson and Gina A. Zurlo, *World Christian Encyclopedia*, 3rd ed. (Edinburgh: Edinburgh University Press, 2019), 29; technical notes on p. 965. The method for calculating this is described in Todd M. Johnson and Kenneth R. Ross, *Atlas of Global Christianity* (Edinburgh: Edinburgh University Press, 2009), 316–17.

interaction, we are limited in our ability to even begin to give witness to adherents of another religion. There is no personal access.

Besides being found imbedded in unreached people groups or insulated in other religions, there is one other arena in which those without access to the Bible, to a church, and to known believers are found.

Inhabiting Gospel-Restricted Locales

A final category to consider when determining where the unreached are located has to do with geography. As mentioned earlier, the definition we are using for unreached peoples is taken from David Platt. Here it is again: "Unreached peoples and places are those among whom Christ is largely unknown and the church is relatively insufficient to make Christ known in its broader population without outside help." Notice that unreached locales (places) are part of the definition. Platt sums up the reason for that inclusion as follows:

> Biblical mission strategy should focus on both peoples and places where Christ is largely unknown and the church is relatively insufficient to make Christ known in its broader population without outside help. As followers of Christ in the church, we must send and go as missionaries to unreached places around the world. We should also send and go as missionaries to more reached places with a significant population of unreached peoples. And we should intentionally work in more reached places that have significant potential for reaching unreached peoples and places.[15]

There are vast geographic regions where Christ is largely unknown. Many of these are designated "restricted access nations"—i.e., countries whose governments forbid the propagation of the gospel, along with the entrance of gospel-bearing messengers. Some of the most restricted are North Korea, Afghanistan, Somalia, Libya, Pakistan, Saudi Arabia, Eritrea, Sudan, Yemen, Iran, India, and China.[16] The sources of restriction include communism, Islamic oppression, and Hindu fundamentalism. These are places where many of A Third of Us reside.

Fortunately, the barriers of geography in our modern globalized world have somewhat diminished. One the one hand, there has been an acceleration of global communications and internet capability, which have

---

15 Platt, "Rethinking Unreached Peoples."

16 "The World Watch: The Top 50 Countries Where It's Most Difficult to Follow Jesus," Open Doors website, https://www.opendoorsusa.org/christian-p/ersecution/world-watch-list/.

given ability to penetrate highly restricted areas. The gospel can be broadcast and/or narrowcast into regions that formerly were inaccessible. However, the challenge of personal follow-up remains, making these technological means helpful, but inadequate by themselves.

On the other hand, today there are more movements of peoples beyond their traditional homelands than ever before. Migration, which is caused by numerous factors and is both global and local in scope, has resulted in the ability for Christians to meet otherwise unreached peoples as they come into areas where Christians are present. We no longer need to rely solely on strategies and structures that assume fixed, isolated people groups. But in the end, without a visible indigenous church within the ethnic homeland, no people group will have the ability to evangelize itself and become "reached." Thus, the need for the presence of believers in a given locale.

Is My Unsaved Neighbor "Unreached"?

A retired high school teacher who had spent his career teaching in a midsize town in the Midwest said to me, "I recall when I was still teaching that I had some students pass through my classes who didn't know the gospel. They didn't have an inkling about who Jesus is. So there are unreached people right next door, right?"

This reflects a common misconception about what is meant by "unreached." When we meet those in our community who are unsaved, it's easy to assume that they are also unreached—equating "unsaved" with "unreached." However, that is not the case. This is an easy misunderstanding of the terms that needs clarification.

We can say with confidence that everyone in communities across North America is "reached" with the gospel. This means that they all have access, in some form or another, to the gospel. Access to the gospel gives them opportunity. They have the opportunity to believe it, reject it, or ignore it. The bottom line is that they have access to it. Besides encounters with believers, the good news of Jesus can be accessed daily via television, radio, internet, published books, and pamphlets. Online digital evangelism is

> When we meet those in our community who are unsaved, it's easy to assume that they are also unreached—equating "unsaved" with "unreached."

occurring nonstop. More recently, as a result of the coronavirus pandemic, online church services are accessible by the thousands.

But that's not all. Throughout the US alone there are more than 385,000 churches, most of which preach and teach the gospel, where the story of Jesus can be heard and learned. Additionally, the Bible is not only available but can be found in over one hundred different versions or "specialty editions." Along many of our highways, giant billboards proclaim some variety of evangelistic message that can't be missed. Most important, however, is that born-again believers, who can point a seeker to Christ, can be encountered readily in most every community.

Across North America, the three "nos" do not exist. There are Bibles in abundance, believers galore, and churches aplenty. These realities add up to full access to the gospel. Although many remain unrepentant, no one is unreached. Everyone has access and opportunity to encounter the gospel and become a follower of Christ.

Mrs. Taufik, on the other hand, has none of these. Mrs. Taufik remains unreached. Mrs. Taufik remains un-accessed. Mrs. Taufik awaits the proclamation of the gospel—along with the other 3.2 billion people who comprise A Third of Us.

REACHING A THIRD OF US

Through the centuries, the church has engaged in the task of world evangelization by sending out hundreds of thousands of missionaries and expending billions upon billions of dollars. Even with all of that, however, the task is far from complete, as 3.2 billion people are still unreached. When understood from the three "nos"—no believers, no Bible, and no church—it is obvious that much remains to be done.

The unreached are found in three broad categories: *imbedded in unreached people groups, insulated in other religions, and inhabiting gospel-restricted locales.* It is up to us to provide access to the gospel to the billions who comprise A Third of Us.

CHAPTER 2

The Priority of Jesus' Last Words

"If you love me, you will keep my commandments."

—*Jesus*

J esus' last words should be our first priority! Think about it for a moment. The last words of a departing loved one are always taken seriously. This is especially true if that person is saying farewell for the very final time. When those words contain instruction about a pressing and dear matter, the departing one will take extraordinary measures to convey them. It isn't unusual to find those words to be profound and even provocative. When they are, they have usually been well thought-out and masterfully crafted beforehand. They are often written in a "last will and testament" to assure they will be accurately carried out once the person has passed on. Those final words often convey precious and pressing matters to the one who is leaving.

In the days following his resurrection, Jesus met with his disciples on several different occasions. You'll recall reading in the Gospels about him meeting them in a room in Jerusalem, on a mountainside in Galilee, by the Sea of Galilee, and on the slopes of the Mount of Olives. He met with his disciples at several different times and in a variety of places in order that he might impart to them final instructions that were crucially important. The reaching of lost souls depended upon them.

> ## Jesus' last words should be our first priority!

To be sure, during his post-resurrection appearances, Jesus passed along other information to his disciples as well. But his final days with them were bookended with instruction about the upcoming global outreach they were to inaugurate. He first told them about it on the evening of Resurrection Day. He last instructed them forty days later, just moments before his ascension into heaven.

Throughout history these passages have been given various labels. The most common has been *commission*. This word is found in the passage titles of Matthew 28 in most Bibles, with the adjective *great* modifying it. Another term that has been used to emphasize the importance of these passages is *mandate*. Some have said these passages comprise the church's "marching orders." Others have called them "the divine charter of Christian missions."[17] No matter the preferred nomenclature, the importance of these passages—revealing the global outreach of the church—cannot be missed.

---

17 George Peters, in *A Biblical Theology of Missions* (212), seems to prefer this term because it gives the charter to the church's responsibility in her outward relationship.

The Great Commission Passages

The final chapter of three of the Gospels, and the next to last chapter of John, along with the first chapter of Acts, record Jesus' final discourses with the disciples. Within these chapters we discover what has come to be known as his five "Great Commission" statements. If one were to read them starting with Matthew's Gospel, the following is the order in which they appear in the New Testament.

Matthew 28:18–20

And Jesus came and said to them, *"All authority in heaven and on earth has been given to me. Go therefore and make disciples of all nations, baptizing them in the name of the Father and of the Son and of the Holy Spirit, teaching them to observe all that I have commanded you. And behold, I am with you always, to the end of the age."*

Mark 16:15

And he said to them, *"Go into all the world and proclaim the gospel to the whole creation."*

Luke 24:44–49

Then he said to them, *"These are my words that I spoke to you while I was still with you, that everything written about me in the Law of Moses and the Prophets and the Psalms must be fulfilled."* Then he opened their minds to understand the Scriptures, and said to them, *"Thus it is written, that the Christ should suffer and on the third day rise from the dead, and that repentance for the forgiveness of sins should be proclaimed in his name to all nations, beginning from Jerusalem. You are witnesses of these things. And behold, I am sending the promise of my Father upon you. But stay in the city until you are clothed with power from on high."*

John 20:21–23

Jesus said to them again, *"Peace be with you. As the Father has sent me, even so I am sending you."* And when he had said this, he breathed on them and said to them, *"Receive the Holy Spirit. If you forgive the sins of any, they are forgiven them; if you withhold forgiveness from any, it is withheld."*

15

Acts 1:7–8

> He said to them, *"It is not for you to know times or seasons that the Father has fixed by his own authority. But you will receive power when the Holy Spirit has come upon you, and you will be my witnesses in Jerusalem and in all Judea and Samaria, and to the end of the earth."*

Putting the Passages in Chronological Order

One of the most common mistakes made when reading through the Gospels is to treat these passages as though they were synoptic, meaning "to view as the same." Or to put it differently, to see these passages as given at one time, conveying the same thought but from different angles. Many harmonies of the Gospels misleadingly construct them as such.

However, a closer look at the context surrounding these passages reveals otherwise. This is important to remember when reaching A Third of Us. Upon examination of the contexts and settings where Jesus conveyed them, it becomes apparent that Jesus gave these statements to his disciples on five different occasions, in five different addresses, at five different geographical settings, with five different emphases.

That being the case, it is evident that these statements are sequential rather than synoptic. Chronologically, Jesus gave them in an order much different from the biblical order in which one finds them when starting with Matthew. As was already mentioned, noting the contexts surrounding these passages reveals the true order in which Jesus gave them. Let's take a look.

On the evening of Resurrection Day, Jesus met with ten distraught disciples in a room in Jerusalem (John 20:19). For reasons we do not know, Thomas was absent; and Judas had taken his life, resulting in only ten disciples present. At that meeting Jesus gave the briefest of the commissions, found in John 20:21–23.

Eight days later (John 20:26), when Thomas was present and there were eleven disciples, Jesus gave the added information found in Mark 16:15–18. About a week or so following that, he met with the disciples a third time, after they had walked all the way to Galilee to meet with him there. It was there that Jesus gave the most detailed of the commissions, recorded in Matthew 28:18–20. Approximately two weeks later, after the disciples had returned to Jerusalem and on the eve of his ascension, Jesus gave the Luke

24:44–49 commission.[18] Finally, possibly after an interval of only a few short hours, Jesus gave his farewell address, recorded in Acts 1:7–8.

Thus, the chronological order in which Jesus gave the "Great Commission" was as follows:

John 20:21–23
    Mark 16:15
        Matthew 28:18–20
            Luke 24:44–49
                Acts 1:7–8

|———————————————————————————————————→

Resurrection   **Forty days**   **Ascension**

Why This Order?

Why would Jesus have given his disciples the mandate to reach all nations in this order? There are several considerations that help make sense of this number and order. We need to consider the tension of those days and the fragile emotional state of the disciples.

Jesus wanted to incrementally impart information to the disciples about their next assignment so they could adequately grasp and comprehend it. Incremental information, the process of adding a little more detail at each successive setting, allowed the disciples time to slowly digest the essence of what Jesus was conveying to them. This was to be a lifelong task in which they were being instructed. It would have global significance. They needed to get it right.

During their three years with him, Jesus had the disciples periodically engage in restrictive outreaches. Those outreaches were limited in time, scope, and message. Now all that was going to change. A greater mission awaited them. By conveying his instructions in incremental stages, Jesus was giving them time to decipher and comprehend the magnitude of the task he was leaving them to do.

---

18 The timing of Luke's commission is the most difficult to ascertain. However, most commentators would agree that there is a division of time between Luke 24:43 and what follows, starting with verse 44. A reading of the text would suggest that verses 44–49 would have taken place back in Jerusalem after the disciples had met with Jesus in Galilee. In commenting on this section from Luke, Alexander Bruce states, "It is at this point, if anywhere, that room must be made for an extended period of occasional intercourse between Jesus and His disciples. It is conceivable that what follows refers to another occasion" (*The Expositor's Greek Testament*, 650). Henry Alford agrees, with the added emphasis that these words "cannot have been said *on this evening*; for after the command in verse 49, the disciples would not have gone away into Galilee (673).

The disciples were in no frame of mind to absorb the full measure of instruction in one sitting. The recent events of Jesus' trials, death and resurrection had left them traumatized! They were in a state of uncertainty and confusion. They were in no condition to comprehend the details of this new assignment. Therefore, Jesus wisely spoon-fed the information to them bit-by-bit, so they would be capable of digesting it.

By teaching through repetition, Jesus was emphasizing its importance. He was showing them how crucial to the plan of redemption their new task really was. Just as a parent warns or instructs a child several times about an important matter so that its seriousness is captured, so Jesus employed this pedagogical method to impress upon the disciples the importance of their next task.

The following chart demonstrates the progressive and incremental elements of Jesus' Great Commission statements.

Passage	Location	When	To Whom	Mandate	Emphasis
John 20:21–23	Jerusalem	Evening of Resurrection Day	Ten disciples	"As the Father has sent me, …"	The Model
Mark 16:15	Jerusalem	Eight days later	Eleven disciples	"Go into all the world … to the whole creation."	The Magnitude
Matthew 28:18–20	Mountain in Galilee	Between one and two weeks later	Eleven disciples	"… make disciples of all nations …"	The Method
Luke 24:44–49	Jerusalem	About forty days after the resurrection	Eleven disciples	"… repentance for the forgiveness of sins should be proclaimed …"	The Message
Acts 1:8	Mount of Olives	Forty days after the resurrection	Eleven disciples	"you will receive power …Jerusalem, Judea, Samaria…"	The Means

It is clear that Jesus did not give the Great Commission to the disciples all in one sitting. This was too important a task to be handled so quickly. There was too much of a chance for misunderstanding. There was too much detail to be absorbed. There was the risk that it would not have become a priority to them, and consequently they would never have accomplished it. For the sake of clarity, Jesus had to give it over and over and over again.

Relationship between the Great Commission and Personal Commissions

Are there other *Great Commission* passages in Scripture, other than these five that I have mentioned? No, there are not. Nevertheless, we do know of other divinely given *personal* commissions to individual messengers in New Testament times. None of them, however, were addressed to the whole church. They were limited by either time, scope, or the individual's personal involvement. It is clear that each of these personal commissions perfectly aligned with the overriding mandates found in the Great Commission passages.

The book of Acts presents us with some excellent examples of personal commissions. Philip was given a commission to go evangelize an influential Ethiopian (Acts 8:26–29), Ananias of Damascus was commissioned to reach out to Saul (Acts 9:10–16), Peter was commissioned to go meet Cornelius and his relatives and close friends (Acts 10:19–20), and Paul was given a commission to evangelize Gentiles (Acts 26:16–18). While the others were given time-limited assignments, Paul's commission was for life. Today God continues to give such commissions to individual Christians so that the unreached may be reached.

It is Paul's personal commission that is the most intriguing and helpful to us as we seek to engage A Third of Us. Although given directly by Jesus at the time of Paul's conversion, it wasn't until twenty-five years later that Paul revealed its specific content. And instead of telling the churches about it (at least in writing), we find it in Acts 26:14–18 as part of Paul's legal defense before King Agrippa.

> And when we had all fallen to the ground, I heard a voice saying to me in the Hebrew language, *"Saul, Saul, why are you persecuting me? It is hard for you to kick against the goads."* And I said, *"Who are you, Lord?"* And the

Lord said, *"I am Jesus whom you are persecuting. But rise and stand upon your feet, for I have appeared to you for this purpose, to appoint you as a servant and witness to the things in which you have seen me and to those in which I will appear to you, delivering you from your people and from the Gentiles—to whom I am sending you to open their eyes, so that they may turn from darkness to light and from the power of Satan to God, that they may receive forgiveness of sins and a place among those who are sanctified by faith in me."*

This is one of the most beautiful and exacting commissions ever given to an individual—one every message-bearer could wish to have. Jesus told Paul that he was sending him out as a pioneer missionary. Included in Paul's commission are some basic elements:

> **The combined Great Commission passages are the "mother ship" commissions addressed to the whole church for reaching the unreached.**

1. The sender: "I am Jesus whom you are persecuting.... I am sending you ... "
2. The sent one: "Saul, Saul, ... I am sending you ... "
3. Those to whom he is sent: " ... the Gentiles—to whom I am sending you ... "
4. His assignment: " ... to open their eyes, so that they may turn from darkness to light and from the power of Satan to God, that they may receive forgiveness of sins and a place among those who are sanctified by faith in me."

Is this a genuine missionary commission? Absolutely. Is it on par with the Great Commission passages? No, it is not, since it has built-in limitations, whereas the Great Commission does not. Paul's commission was personal, but not universal.

So it is with other personal commissions, or "missionary calls," that Jesus loves giving to willing and receptive hearts. Perhaps you have experienced one yourself. They can be direct, jolting, passionate, and unquestionably clear. Yet none of them—not even Paul's—are to be placed on par with the Great Commission. The combined Great Commission passages are the "mother ship" commissions addressed to the whole church for reaching the unreached. Out of them, all personal commissions, or "missionary calls" (as they are sometimes called), are launched, and so, consequently, dependent on them.

What becomes fascinating, when spending time in these passages, is to discover how they each contain ingredients necessary for successful outreach. This holds true today, as we focus our outreach on a third of the world's population—3.2 billion people—who do not have access to the gospel.

REACHING A THIRD OF US

The Great Commission passages record the parting words of Jesus. By them he addressed the pressing matter of spreading his good news to the nations. This is something the disciples were to inaugurate. It was something they were to be engaged in after he departed.

Methodically, one by one, Jesus relayed to them the essence of their task. He met with them at five different times in five different settings to give them five different components of his mission. He passed these messages along to them incrementally so they would be able to grasp the progression and importance of this teaching.

Jesus would give personal commissions to particular followers as well. But each of them would be tied to, and fall in line with, the five mission addresses given to the disciples. Without question, these five mission statements of Jesus make up the missional Magna Carta of the church: from its inception, for today, and into the future.

CHAPTER 3

Our Model for Reaching

*"If you don't believe the messenger,
you won't believe the message."*

—James M. Kouzes and Barry Z. Posner

Over and over again, throughout history, God has shown himself to be a missionary God. As such, he has little problem sending anyone anywhere at any time. For the benefit of his plans and will, he sends people from where they are to where he needs them to be so that his divine purposes might be accomplished and his name most glorified, and this certainly includes the seeking and saving of lost, unreached peoples.

Scriptures abound with stories of God sending people on mission. Whenever he had an important task to accomplish, he sent someone to get it done. He sent Noah and his family into the ark to save mankind from the flood. He sent Abraham from Ur to the land of Canaan. He sent Jacob to Haran and back to preserve the Jewish bloodline. He sent Joseph into Egypt, Moses from the desert of Midian to the court of Pharaoh, the Israelites out of Egypt, Jonah to Nineveh, and Daniel to Babylon, to name just a few.

> As part of that process to transmit the good news of redemption throughout the world, Jesus sent out the disciples by way of his Great Commission statements. The people of God have been on mission ever since.

Then, when it came time to fulfill his redemptive plan, he sent his son, Jesus, from heaven to earth, the wise men to Bethlehem, and Joseph and Mary to Egypt and back. Some years later, he sent John the Baptist to prepare the way for Jesus' public ministry. After Jesus' ministry was complete, God sent the Holy Spirit to the church, and then the church into the world.

As part of that process to transmit the good news of redemption throughout the world, Jesus sent out the disciples by way of his Great Commission statements. The people of God have been on mission ever since. The living God is indeed a missionary God![19] What does it mean to be sent on mission? Whether a diplomatic, business, or religious mission, the term *mission* presupposes four necessary components. Every mission entails 1) a sender, 2) a person sent, 3) those to whom one is sent, and 4) an assignment. The entire process presumes that the one doing the sending has the authority to do so.[20]

---

19 The statement "The Living God Is a Missionary God" comes from the title of John Stott's article in *Perspectives on the World Christian Movement*, 3–9.

20 See *Transforming Mission*, pages 1–2, where David Bosch makes the argument that these four components are a logically necessary part of any sending, not only from without but also from within the church.

We read at the end of each Gospel that the disciples didn't have a clue as to what Jesus was going to ask of them next. They didn't have an inkling that he was going to send them on a global mission that was in turn to be picked up and carried on by all believers who would come after them. So, following his death and resurrection, Jesus repeatedly made contact with his disciples to pass that information along.

Jesus Meets the Disciples

Following Jesus' crucifixion, the disciples hid themselves away in a room somewhere in Jerusalem. It was dangerous for them, as Jesus' followers, to be out and about on the streets. The room they were hiding in could well have been the same room in which they had celebrated the Passover together just days earlier. But whether or not it was the same place, Jesus knew where they were and made a stunning appearance. He suddenly appeared unannounced in their midst, even though they were tucked behind closed doors (John 20:19).

Jesus wasted no time telling his disciples of their next assignment. The first hint that he wanted them to engage in a global-wide endeavor that would take them out of the confines of Israel took place that evening—the same day as his resurrection. In this first post-resurrection meeting with them, Jesus mentioned the bare essence of their new assignment. To be sure, his words were brief. But enough was said to get them thinking about what they were to do next.

Jesus said to them again, *"Peace be with you. As the Father has sent me, even so I am sending you."* John 20:21

Have you ever thought about what Jesus did not include in this brief commission? He did not tell them where they were to go, how far they were to go, how long they were to go, why they were to go, nor the specifics of the message they were to take with them. Instead, Jesus' objective at this point was simply to inform them that they were being sent to do something different from what had been done in the past.

Peace and Mission

However, before Jesus could even begin to hint to the disciples that he had a new plan for them, he first had to set their minds at ease. They had gathered that evening behind closed doors because they were afraid that their enemies might discover them. As followers of a recently condemned criminal, they had good reason to fear for their lives. If their leader, in a flash, could be unjustly tried, condemned, and executed, so could they. It was dangerous for them to be identified by anyone outside of their tiny circle.

Once they had gathered together, they marveled at the strange messages they received throughout the day from several individuals claiming that Jesus had been seen alive. While they were discussing the validity of those reports, Jesus suddenly appeared in their midst.

> In a world full of uncertainty, messengers of Christ are to possess the peace of Christ, for their very task is to present to the world the Prince of Peace.

Jesus knew that this would be a difficult teachable moment. In their present state of mind, the disciples were not prepared to process the mind-boggling reports they had been hearing, let alone accept new teaching from him. These traumatized men were mentally and emotionally exhausted. They were brokenhearted, disappointed, and direction-less all at the same time. With their leader unexpectedly executed, their plans had been shattered and their dreams of future greatness had been destroyed. They had lost everything—or at least so they supposed. In the midst of this confusion, Jesus stands among them and calmly says, "Peace be with you."

Jesus was well aware that his first task was to restore their mental and emotional equilibrium. He probably spoke even more words of reassurance to them than John recorded, but these are the ones that stood out when he wrote his Gospel decades later. These words of reassurance and confidence were just what the disciples needed at this time of bewilderment. Once calmed, they were prepared to hear what Jesus had to say next.

There is an important lesson for us in these words today. These words of reassurance and peace are as heartening to those who go on mission in this age as they were to the disciples back then. In a world full of uncertainty, messengers of Christ are to possess the peace of Christ, for their very task is to present to the world the Prince of Peace. Those who have experienced peace with God also have the peace of God within themselves. Inner peace of a pardoned sinner grounds the heart for service and witness even in the midst of external turmoil and uncertainty.

Jesus Sends the Disciples

This foreign thrust of going outside the borders of Israel was a seismic change in the way God would now utilize his messengers in reaching the nations. In the Old Testament Israel functioned primarily as a magnet, drawing nations to the light of God through their life experience with him. That drawing is referred to as "centripetal mission," whereby Israel, on the strength of their exemplary reputation and obedience to God, drew peoples of other nations to Jerusalem, to the temple, and ultimately to God.[21] Passages such as Isaiah 60:1–3 were embedded in the minds of the disciples:

Arise, shine, for your light has come, and the glory of the Lord rises upon you. See, darkness covers the earth and thick darkness is over the peoples, but the Lord rises upon you and his glory appears over you. Nations will come to your light, and kings to the brightness of your dawn.

Now Jesus was telling his disciples that the plan had dramatically changed. The missional plan will now be the opposite. Instead of centering their witness in Jerusalem and waiting for the nations to be drawn to them, they were to leave Jerusalem and fan out across the Roman Empire and beyond on a centrifugal, outward mission. This thrusting forth from Jerusalem constituted a huge reversal of tactics; and the disciples understood it. They realized they were being asked to do mission the opposite way of what they had known and seen practiced.

Sent to Send

It is without question that the Father sent Jesus to earth on a mission. Twenty-nine times in the Gospel of John Jesus says that he was here on earth because the Father had sent him. He knew he was here on mission.

Without getting overly technical, it is helpful to understand the words behind the two "sends" found in John 20:21. There are two different words for "send" in Greek, and Jesus uses both in this verse. One, *apostello*, carries the idea of a person being officially sent on a mission that has unquestionable authorization behind it. When defending his authority, Jesus uses this word to relate God's sending of himself fifteen different times in the dialogues found in the Gospel of John.

---

21 For a fuller discussion of the Old Testament concept of centripetal focus and the New Testament concept of the opposite, centrifugal focus, see George Peters, *A Biblical Theology of Missions*, 21–22.

The other word, *pempo*, does not carry so much the meaning of an "official delegate" or "authorized sent one." It has more to do with the sending process—like when one pushes the "send" button on an email message. In the Gospel of John, Jesus uses this word in reference to himself being sent by the Father twenty-four different times. His choice of the words depended upon the emphasis he was making.

However, there are times when both words are found coupled together in the same sentence. When they are, the force of the authorized mission (*apostello*) is imposed on the second word (*pempo*). John 7:28–29 is a good example. This coupled usage of the two words is how Jesus purposefully expressed his commission in John 20:21. The verse literally reads,

> "As the father has officially sent me on an authorized mission (apostello), even so I am sending (pempo) you out."

In other words, Jesus wanted his disciples to clearly understand that he was now propelling them forth—like an instantly released email, but at the same level of authorization by which he himself had been sent. By using these two words, the right to go forward was not lost on the disciples. Christ does not merely leave his disciples in the world; he sends them into it. Jesus was giving them authority to not only go reach the unreached, but that those who follow after them would keep on going as well.[22]

Three Transmissions—Same Authority

The authority behind reaching unreached peoples starts and ends with Almighty God.

As I mentioned earlier, the sending on any kind of a mission—whether diplomatic, business, or religious—presumes that the one doing the sending has the authority to do so. John 20:21 reveals where the authority for the sending of believers originates. It starts with God the Father, who, as creator of the universe by fiat, has the sovereign right to send.

The authority behind reaching unreached peoples starts and ends with Almighty God. It has its origin in God the Father. It is transmitted to the disciples through Jesus the Son, then is vicariously passed on by the disciples through the Spirit to believers in each subsequent generation.

22 The tense of the first "sent" (*apostello*) is aorist, showing an action once taken and not to be repeated. Jesus was sent only once into the world to provide salvation for mankind. The second "send" (*pempo*) is present tense, something that keeps going on, intended to show a sending that keeps going until the job is completed.

Father ⇨ Son ⇨ Disciples ⇨ Church

Authority

This mandate to the church did not originate in any church council, by papal edict, or at an ecclesiastic assembly. The missional outreach of the church originated in the eternal will of God the Father, proceeded through the historical mission of the Son while in the world, was passed along to the disciples, and subsequently flows to every generation of believers by the presence of the Holy Spirit. Our mission is ongoing and grounded in divine authority. This gives us confidence that all the efforts undertaken to reach A Third of Us are divinely sanctioned.

Modeling the Way

An important trait of effective leaders is that they are models in life and practice to those who know them. Effective leaders model the ideals they desire their followers to emulate. By their conduct, they establish the standards which constituents, peers, and colleagues are expected to follow. By their example, they also establish the pace and manner in which organizational goals are pursued. Through modeling the way, a leader sets the bar of excellence others are expected to reach.[23] By way of his life and ministry, Jesus set the standard for how his followers are to conduct themselves while engaged in the task of carrying the gospel to the world. His life became the impeccable model for everything: character, morals, ethical behavior, etc. By emulating his life, followers of Jesus will never need to question whether their conduct is consistent with the gospel they proclaim.

However, a word of caution is necessary and important if we are determined to duplicate the life and ministry of Jesus. Although some say it is incumbent on Jesus' messengers to define their ministry by his example, this can never be fully achieved. Jesus is an impossible model to replicate perfectly! No person today can declare or define his or her ministry as Jesus did in Luke 4:18: "The Spirit of the Lord is upon me, because he has anointed

---

23 One of the best books on leadership practices is *The Leadership Challenge*, by Kouzes and Posner, who state that modeling the way is the first of five basic leadership practices of a good leader.

29

me to proclaim good news to the poor. He has sent me to proclaim liberty to the captives and recovering of sight to the blind, to set at liberty those who are oppressed."[24] Only he could do those sorts of things.

Therefore, because of Jesus' unique personhood and mission, the disciples could not perfectly model their ministries after his. Neither can we. Stop and think for a moment about Jesus' unique salvific mission: 1) he was born to die for the sins of the world (Luke 19:10); 2) he confined his mission to the Jewish people (Matt 10:5–6); and 3) he performed unique, miraculous "signs" and "wonders" that were meant to authenticate and separate his mission from all others (John 2:11; 4:54; 7:31).[25]

How could one begin to think that he or she could or should match that? There is a huge distinction between Jesus' mission and our mission. If we don't recognize this, we are doomed to deviate from what Jesus really would have us to be doing. Some go so far as to say that those who don't distinguish the work of Jesus from that which he gave to his disciples cannot be credible.[26]

Jesus models the way for his ambassadors through his human attributes. The life of Jesus as a person is the same life that should be lived by all Christ-followers.

This whole discussion begs the next logical question. If Christ-followers are unable to copy Jesus in what was his unique mission to the world, then in what way are they to emulate him? The answer is found in the example of Jesus. Jesus models the way for his ambassadors through his human attributes. The life of Jesus as a person is the same life that should be lived by all Christ-followers. It is possible, then, to consider Jesus the prototype that the rest of us should follow.[27] Following his lead in matters pertaining to his humanity should be every worker's goal.

24 This is what was asserted by James Engel and William Dyrness when they mistakenly chose to ignore the Great Commission passages and land on Luke 4:18–19 as the defining passage for mission both in Jesus' ministry and for all missionaries today. Their error of ignoring the obvious, clear Great Commission mission passages and elevating the obscure is a classical hermeneutical mistake that finds little justification.

25 Andreas J. Kostenberger and Peter T. O'Brien, *Salvation to the Ends of the Earth*, 169ff.

26 Christopher Little, "What Makes Mission Christian?" *International Journal of Frontier Missiology*, April–June 2008: 65–73.

27 In Hebrews 3:1, Jesus is called "the apostle and high priest of our confession." An apostle is one who is sent on an official mission—in our terms, a "missionary," the Latin equivalent and translation of the word *apostle*. Therefore, Jesus himself is called a missionary in the New Testament.

"As ... So ..."

In John 20:21, the two conjunctions, *as* and *so*, show by comparison how one can follow Jesus' model in personal conduct and public ministry. The word *as* (*kathos*) means "in like manner." The solemn teaching of Jesus is that his messengers are to manifest his life and character "in like manner" in their ministries as well. Just as Jesus manifested the character of God to the world, believers are to bear that same kind of witness in life as they minister.

Look again at Jesus' statement in John 20:21: "As the Father has sent me, even so I am sending you." Consider the following thirteen statements that Jesus made about himself during his lifetime, which we as his servants should model in our calling to reach the unreached.

Mission: *"For the Son of Man came to seek and to save the lost"* *(Luke 19:10) "... so I am sending you."*

Motivation: *"I work for the honor and glory of the one who sent me"* *(John 7:18; paraphrased) "... so I am sending you."*

Objective: *"I came that they may have life and have it abundantly"* *(John 10:10) "... so I am sending you."*

Offer: *"Come to me, all who labor and are heavy laden, and I will give you rest"* *(Matt 11:28) "... so I am sending you."*

Focus: *"I came not to call the righteous, but sinners (to repentance)"* *(Matt 9:13) "... so I am sending you."*

Will: *"For I have come down from heaven, not to do my own will but the will of him who sent me." (John 4:38) "... so I am sending you."*

Teamwork: *"And he appointed twelve (whom he also named apostles) so that they might be with him and he might send them out to preach"* *(Mark 3:14) "... so I am sending you."*

Servanthood: *"the Son of Man came not to be served but to serve ... "* *(Matt 20:28) "... so I am sending you."*

Personality: *"learn from me, for I am gentle and lowly in heart ... "* *(Matt 11:29) "... so I am sending you."*

Approval: *"I always do the things that are pleasing to him"* *(John 8:29) "... so I am sending you."*

Ownership: *"the Son of Man has nowhere to lay his head"*
(Matt 8:20) "… so I am sending you."

Compassion: *"When he saw the crowds, he had compassion for them, because they were harassed and helpless, like sheep without a shepherd"*
(Matt 9:36) "… so I am sending you."

Finishing Well: *"I glorified you on earth, having accomplished the work that you gave me to do" (John 17:4) "… so I am sending you."*

The Right to Speak

Jesus deliberately made his mission the model of what ours ought to be. What he portrayed in life and practice his servants are to do as they reach the unreached. The model of Jesus is the rod by which all personal conduct and ministry activities are to be measured. We gain the right to speak based on the right life from which we speak. Our lifestyle is right if it is modeled after Christ's. People will believe the message because they believe the messenger.

> The first priority of the church is not to spread the gospel of Jesus Christ. The first priority of the church is to make it worthy to spread the gospel of Jesus Christ. —Tozer

A. W. Tozer once said, "The first priority of the church is not to spread the gospel of Jesus Christ. The first priority of the church is to make it worthy to spread the gospel of Jesus Christ." That is why Count Nicholas Zinzendorf, the founder of the Moravians, one of the earliest and largest mission movements in Germany, could declare, "I have one passion—it is he, it is he alone!"

When a clothing designer wants to model her new apparel, she does it in one of two ways. One way is by putting the new designs on human-like mannequins for display. With this method, people must go to a store to discover the new designs for themselves. Another way is for the designer to put her new designs on living models. The models then show them off by walking a central runway that extends right into the midst of an audience.

Christ's ambassadors display his attributes by both methods. The conduct of those on Jesus' mission can't be missed, as they are constantly on display "walking the runway" among watching peoples. If they are unimpressed with the life of the messenger, they will be unimpressed with the message.

REACHING A THIRD OF US

In his first Great Commission statement to his disciples, Jesus focused on the very meaning of mission—that of being sent. God's design for reaching the nations has now been completely reversed. Up till that time, the nations were to go to Israel to discover God and his salvation. But starting with the disciples, the church now has the task of taking that knowledge to the nations.

Jesus made it clear that the authority behind the mission is given by God himself. This makes the right and the responsibility of engaging in missional outreach unquestionable. How were they personally to engage in that mission? By following the ministry model set by Jesus himself.

In regard to timing, Jesus gave this first commission to the disciples on the evening of Resurrection Day. From that time onward, the disciples knew that things were going to be different. Although details were sketchy, they realized they were being sent out to do something totally different from the past. They would be "turning the world upside down" (Acts 17:6).

CHAPTER 4

The Magnitude of Reaching

"To know the will of God we need an open Bible and an open map." —William Carey

J esus met with the disciples a second time in another surprise visit. It was eight days later at a rented room somewhere in Jerusalem. It may have been the same place as his first post-resurrection encounter with them the week before. The location isn't as important as what took place.

By comparing John 20:24–29 with Mark 16:15, we know Jesus had a couple of objectives for meeting with them this second time. One was to reassure Thomas, who was absent from the previous meeting, that he really was alive and well. The other was to impart additional information to each of the disciples about the task ahead of them. Eleven disciples were present, as Judas, the traitor, did not survive the events of Passion Week.

The disciples, having had a week to mull over their first encounter with Jesus, seem to have been as unprepared for this second encounter as they were the first. The Gospel writer Mark states that they were eating together when he appeared in their midst (Mark 16:14). Startled by his sudden entry through locked doors, Jesus immediately calmed their nerves by saying, "Peace be with you" (John 20:26).

Just what had the disciples been discussing among themselves before Jesus' arrival? Besides the grandeur of the resurrection itself, no doubt the other hot topic must have been the implications to them personally of Jesus' announcement the previous week that they were now being sent somewhere. But to where and to whom they were going was left unclear; and equally puzzling was what exactly they were to do when they went.

So, at this second encounter, Jesus was more specific about the mission. He knew that the emotional shock of his death, burial, and resurrection was beginning to subside. They could now think more coherently. They were in a better state of mind to receive additional information even though there was still some unbelief on their part (verse 14). He used this time with them to convey two additional pieces of information: 1) the magnitude of the task ahead of them; and 2) the overall goal of their mission.

Into All the World

Once the disciples had calmed, Jesus revealed his wounds to a doubting Thomas who, in return, responded in belief (John 20:26–28). This special, personal attention to Thomas was to become significant to reaching far-away unreached peoples, as we will later see.

Jesus then turned his attention to all eleven disciples, giving them the second installment of his commission. The apostle Peter, who was the eyewitness source behind Mark's Gospel account, remembers Jesus' command as follows: "Go into

Jesus used two phrases that showed the disciples the largeness or magnitude of the task ahead of them: "into all the world" and "to the whole creation."

all the world and proclaim the gospel to the whole creation" (Mark 16:15).

Jesus used two phrases that showed the disciples the largeness or magnitude of the task ahead of them: "into all the world" and "to the whole creation." Their minds must have reeled as they contemplated the enormity of the task! Jesus had said some challenging things to them in the past, but now their new mission was to include the entire world and the entire creation? How could that possibly be?

Jesus' use of the word *all* is significant. When I was a seminary student, I recall a professor telling the class that when you encounter the word *all* in Scripture, be assured that "all means all and that's all all means." Jesus' inclusion of *all* was showing both an extent and a vast inclusiveness.

The word behind *all* in "all the world" is the word *hapas*, which is all-inclusive every time it is used. Jesus is making it clear to his disciples that they are to cover the entire earth with the gospel. Every part of the globe was to hear this good news. No continent was to be excluded; no geographical region ignored. No distance was to be considered too far and no people group too remote. The whole earth was to be covered with the message of Jesus' redemption—the good news, or "gospel." Their task was nothing short of the global reaching of unreached peoples, encompassing the whole world!

To the Whole Creation

The second indication of the enormity of the task was Jesus' command to reach the "whole creation." The word behind whole is the Greek word *pasa*, which more precisely translates "every," or "each one." Some English versions more accurately translate it so.

The point Jesus is making is that along with viewing the task as being geographically global, he also wants the disciples to understand it in bite-size portions and individually. People everywhere are to be presented with the gospel on a personal basis by themselves, by families, or by groups. Just as "all the world" shows that the task is nothing short of global in extension, so "to the whole creation" shows that it is nothing short of an "each person" inclusion. Messengers of Christ are to have a zeal and priority for personal, one-to-one evangelism that reaches to every individual.

Some may ask why Jesus used the words "whole creation" instead of something like "all people" or "each person." Why does he include the full created order in the specific human need of redemption? The answer is not hard to discover. Not only is mankind affected by the fall, but all of creation is as well. It too is in need of redemption (Rom 8:18–22). That doesn't mean we should be preaching to the hills and the trees, to the birds and the animals, for the message is human-specific.

However, creation itself is positively affected too! When fallen human beings get redeemed, their entire worldview changes. Instead of abusing creation, they become aware of making beneficial use of it. In turn, they put into place those practices that better the natural world around them. They become responsible stewards of God's creation. This becomes a natural collateral advantage and benefit in cultures, when people align themselves aright with the Creator of all things. Instead of creation being misused, it gets redeemed through Christ as well.[28] So as people believe and receive the gospel, all of creation gets included in that redemption. The positive effects of human redemption spill over into the entire created order.

Going Green

It is popular today for evangelicals to be involved in the "green movement." Environmental quality and concerns seem to be on everyone's mind. To link those concerns with the Great Commission would help justify engaging in those green activities, making them a legitimate part of mission. So, naturally the question is asked, Does this verse include "eco-justice" as part of the Great Commission mandate?

The answer is yes and no, but more no than yes. No, this is not a part of Christ's mandate by direct order, nor is it what Jesus was teaching here. It would be a stretch to suggest this is what Jesus had in mind when teaching his disciples a week after paying the terrible penalty for man's sin. Humankind's redemption, not creation's renewal, was at the core of this commission.

---

28 Henry Alford, in his commentary *The Greek Testament*, states this about the word creature: "Not to men only, all creation is redeemed by Christ (Col. 1:15, 23): "creature" never appears in the NT to be used of mankind alone. By these words the missionary office is bound upon the church through all ages, till every part of the earth shall have been evangelized"; p. 437.

Evangelization, not beautification, was the goal. The groaning of mankind under the burden of sin (Rom 8:1–4) was the focus, not the groaning of creation under the burden of sinful man (Rom 8:19-22).[29]

> The gospel is only good news if it gets there in time.
> —Carl F. H. Henry

However, although eco-justice is not a part of the church's mission by command, it is a natural by-product of the church's mission by application. The positive effects of human redemption have implications and application to the created world as well. The positive effects of human redemption spill over positively into all of the created world. Through man's belief in Jesus, the world becomes a better, safer, cleaner place in which to live.

World Evangelization

Besides telling his disciples of the enormity of their task in terms of its geographic expansiveness, Jesus took this opportunity to also tell them of the magnitude of their assignment in terms of what was to be the overall goal. Specifically, they were to "proclaim the gospel." This is a strongly specific and evangelistic phrase. Some people, though, are confused about what it means. A closer examination of the phrase helps discover what Jesus intended.

The word *proclaim* is the only imperative in this command of Jesus.[30] Now, we shouldn't get the idea that Jesus was commanding each disciple and every follower after them to become seasoned preachers or expert pulpiteers. Rather, Jesus is emphasizing the duty to outright proclaim the gospel. He wanted to ensure that they understand, just as we should today, that the message of redemption has to be vocalized to people. When these words "proclaim the gospel" are used together, most every time they could and should be translated with the singular word "evangelize."[31]

---

29 For a fuller discussion of how both Catholic and Protestant missions are "greening," see Allan Effa's article, "The Greening of Mission," in *International Bulletin of Missionary Research* vol. 32, no. 4 (October), 2008. The accompanying article, "Missiology in Environmental Context: Tasks for an Ecology of Mission," by Willis Jenkins, is also helpful in seeing the current popular trend of linking eco-mission into the church's mission. Disappointingly, both articles are examples of how the Great Commission passages are ignored in this discussion.

30 Although the word "Go" is important and appears first in the sentence, as an aorist passive participle, it does not carry the force of an imperative, as the word "proclaim" (aorist active imperative) does.

31 Patrick Johnstone, in *The Church Is Bigger Than You Think* (47–48), argues that this passage, as well as others, would be better translated "evangelize." He bemoans the fact that the common Greek form is too often translated "preach the gospel" or "tell the good news," distorting the real force that texts like Mark 16:15 show that the church's real task is to evangelize.

The verse could just as readily read:

"Go into all the world and evangelize the whole creation."

> ## This is the decision we do not make, because it has already been made. Whether we spend our lives for the purpose of reaching all men with the gospel is not optional. Christ has commanded every Christian to do just this. Now there are many different ways of accomplishing this one purpose—but regardless of the particular work God has for each of us to do, the one aim of us all in doing our particular job for the Lord must be the evangelization of the whole world.
>
> —G. Allen Fleece

In mission circles, it is common to speak about three degrees or methods of evangelizing. Evangelism can happen silently through a believer's winsome presence; it can happen by proclamation; or it can happen by persuasive appeal to someone to become a follower Christ.

By his mention of the verb *proclaim* in the imperative, Jesus is discounting the use of believers' "silent presence" as being enough to reach A Third of Us. The world will never be won through the silent presence of Christians, no matter how admirable their conduct may be. Along with a winsome presence must be a vocalization of the message. There must be a conveying of the good news about Jesus, challenging sinners to repent of their sins and place their trust in him for a pardoned life now and eternal life hereafter. Believers are tasked to appropriately proclaim the gospel, with the expectation that some people will listen, be convicted, and ultimately be persuaded to believe.

In 1974, the Billy Graham Evangelistic Association sponsored the International Congress on World Evangelization at Lausanne, Switzerland, which I referred to in chapter 1. That congress formulated the *Lausanne Covenant*, including the following statement regarding "the nature of evangelism," which has been a guidepost in missions ever since.

> *To evangelize is to spread the good news that Jesus Christ died for our sins and was raised from the dead according to the Scriptures, and that as the reigning Lord he now offers the forgiveness of sins and the liberating gifts of the Spirit to all who repent and believe. Our Christian presence in the world is indispensable*

to evangelism, and so is that kind of dialogue whose purpose is to listen sensitively in order to understand. But evangelism itself is the proclamation of the historical, biblical Christ as Saviour and Lord, with a view to persuading people to come to him personally and so be reconciled to God. In issuing the gospel invitation we have no liberty to conceal the cost of discipleship. Jesus still calls all who would follow him to deny themselves, take up their cross, and identify themselves with his new community. The results of evangelism include obedience to Christ, incorporation into his Church and responsible service in the world. (1 Cor 15:3, 4; Acts 2:32–39; John 20:21; 1 Cor 1:23; 2 Cor 4:5; 5:11, 20; Luke 14:25–33; Mark 8:34; Acts 2:40, 47; Mark 10:43–45)[32]

Unquestionably, the overall goal and highest stated priority of Jesus is world evangelization—the kind mentioned in the Lausanne Covenant. Whatever plans, programs, or activities we engage in to reach the unreached, all are to be measured against this priority. As we engage in proclamation, discipleship, church planting, and a host of necessary support ministries, all should promote the progress of world evangelization. There is no nobler goal to which an ambassador of Christ is called; there is no clearer vision that he or she must have. Although a variety of other synonyms and even catchy mottos can be found in definition of the core mission of the church, based on Mark 16:15 it can be said that "world evangelization" states it best. Evangelism should always be considered the lifeblood of outreach to the unreached. The mission of the church has evangelism as its highest priority. Every other activity falls beneath this ultimate goal.

Evangelize!

All five Great Commission passages allude to what is meant by evangelization without directly defining it. When all is considered and taken into account, these passages, along with others, would support a definition of world evangelization as follows:

The process of communicating the gospel of Jesus Christ in culturally sensitive ways, so that all peoples everywhere might have the opportunity to repent of their sins and place their faith in the redemptive work of Jesus for the salvation of their souls.

---

32 Lausanne Covenant, International Congress on World Evangelization, Lausanne, Switzerland, July 16–25, 1974; www.lausanne.org/lausanne-1974/lausanne-covenant.html.

When this is the genuine response, followers of Christ should then commit themselves to becoming his lifelong disciples. The goal of evangelism is to see sinners who are hopelessly lost in their sin accept Christ as their Savior and Lord.

When it comes to world evangelization, let's be realistic as to what is involved. A generation ago, missionary statesman Dick Hillis stated, "It is not our responsibility to bring the world to Christ; but it is our responsibility to take Christ to the world." Only then will A Third of Us be reached.

Every believer should make taking Christ to the world their highest priority, no matter what specific niche of this mission God has entrusted to them. The means employed are many, the methods applied are diverse, the workers sent vary (in race, gender, gifting, training, and skills), and the money expended is enormous. But the overarching goal—world evangelization—is one and the same.

Henry Crocker has portrayed this goal well in his inspirational poem "Evangelize!"

Evangelize!
Give us a watchword for the hour,
A thrilling word, a word of power;
A battle-cry, a flaming breath,
That calls to conquest or to death.

A word to rouse the church from rest,
To heed her Master's high behest;
The call is given: Ye hosts arise,
Our watchword is Evangelize!

The glad evangel now proclaim,
Through all the earth in Jesus' name;
This word is ringing through the skies,
Evangelize! Evangelize!

To dying men, a fallen race,
Make known the gift of Gospel grace;
The world that now in darkness lies,
Evangelize! Evangelize![33]

---

33 https://www.baptistpress.com/resource-library/news/first-person-can-we-talk-about-the-gospel-without-telling-it/.

Determined Thomas

At the beginning of this chapter, we saw Jesus taking time to convince Thomas that he was indeed the risen Lord. Jesus had good reason to focus on Thomas. He foresaw the potential this man had to become one of the most outstanding cross-cultural evangelists among the Eleven.

Thomas, for his part, took every word of Jesus from this encounter to heart. He then acted upon them. From "Doubting Thomas," he was transformed into "Determined Thomas." He was determined to fulfill the mission of Jesus to the extreme extent Jesus had just spoken about.

Not long after Jesus' ascension, Thomas began to make his way eastward. He traveled further and wider than any other apostle. According to church tradition, Thomas crossed countries, kingdoms, continents, and rivers and penetrated diverse religious communities to evangelize unreached peoples. He didn't stop until he reached one of the most remote parts of the earth known to man. He kept on going for thousands of miles until he made his way to what is today southern India, a remarkable journey for that era! There he died a martyr's death, and that is probably the only thing that kept him from going even farther. But he left a trail of believers in his wake! Today, there is an established ancient church in southern India that traces its heritage back to the apostle Thomas.

What drove Thomas to go so far? What motivated him to reach as many people as possible? What transformed him from being doubtful to determined? One single sentence from the mouth of the resurrected Jesus motivated him:

"Go into all the world and proclaim the gospel to the whole creation."
(Mark 16:15)

REACHING A THIRD OF US

The disciples needed to know how important the message of redemption was to all of mankind. They needed to understand that all peoples everywhere were to hear this message. The magnitude of the task was not lost on them. They were to take the gospel into all the world and proclaim the gospel to the whole creation. Both the global extensiveness of the task and the person-by-person "personable-ness" of the task was made clear to them.

World evangelization, the process of communicating the gospel of Jesus Christ in culturally sensitive ways, so that all peoples everywhere might have the opportunity to repent of their sins and place their faith in the redemptive work of Jesus for the salvation of their souls, is the goal of this evangelistic mandate.

Jesus lost one disciple (Judas) during Passion Week, and he didn't want to lose another. He took extra effort to convince Thomas of his resurrection, because he knew the high potential this man had to convince others in faraway places of his saving grace. As it turned out, he was right—Thomas became a bold cross-cultural messenger, taking the gospel to the ends of the earth to reach unreached peoples. Perhaps you too are such a person.

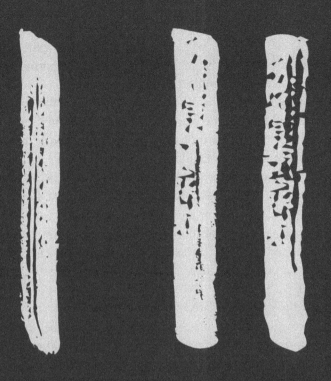

CHAPTER 5

The Method of Reaching Matthew 28:18–20

"Making disciples is far more than a program. It is the mission of our lives. It defines us. A disciple is a disciple maker." —Francis Chan

"Making disciples of Jesus is the overflow of the delight in being disciples of Jesus." —David Platt

R eaching A Third of Us will best happen if we follow the instructions given by Jesus. In this tech-savvy world it is tempting to gravitate toward managerial and technological proficiencies to accomplish the task. Although these can and should be called upon to supplement our efforts, they should never become a substitute for the methodology given by Jesus. He laid out this methodology when he met with the disciples a third time on a mountain in Galilee.

The brief accounts of Jesus' post-resurrection appearances to his disciples cannot include everything Jesus said when he was with them. He likely spent hours speaking to them, mentioning additional things not included in the Gospel records. One of those he likely told the disciples during the encounter mentioned in Mark was that they were to meet him again at a specific mountain in Galilee, just as was preannounced by the angels at the tomb (Matt 28:7).

It would be at least a three-day walk from Jerusalem to get there. So, having two encounters with their resurrected Lord behind them, they left Jerusalem and made their way north to Galilee. They were all too happy to get there. This was their home territory. Every disciple originated from Galilee (Acts 1:11), except Judas. Galilee is the place they most likely would feel safe, away from the hostile environment that still loomed back in Jerusalem because of their connection with the condemned Jesus. The mountain air along with the lapping Sea of Galilee would therapeutically soothe whatever lingering trauma they were experiencing.

The Eleven probably took some time to meet with their families before proceeding to the mountain Jesus had designated for their meeting. Why did Jesus choose this isolated, out-of-the-way place? We often read in the Gospels that when he wanted to impart important instructions to his disciples, he did it in a retreat setting. Many times his place of preference was on a mountain, where they were able to avoid interruptions from the crowds and the distractions of family. In these more intimate settings, Jesus had their undivided attention.

There was good reason why Jesus especially wanted this isolated setting for the next installment of his commission. This was to be the most detailed missional instruction of the five. World evangelization hinged upon them fully comprehending the details he was about to pass along. At this time, he would relate to them the specific methodology he wanted them to follow as they carried the gospel to the ends of the earth. He wanted to make sure they got it right. At this meeting, Jesus was intentional on being exacting as to what their task would entail.

Why was the apostle Matthew the one who recorded this, the most extensive and detailed commission of Jesus? When we recall Matthew's previous profession, the answer is not difficult to discover. Matthew had been a tax collector before becoming a follower of Jesus (Matt 9:9–13; 10:3). As such, he was skilled in keeping records. His livelihood had depended upon accurate bookkeeping. Because of the exactness of details found in this passage, it isn't hard to imagine that Matthew, with parchment and stylus in hand, took notes on what Jesus told the disciples at this gathering. In all likelihood, he kept those notes until a later date, when he would incorporate them into his fuller Gospel.

The Commission That Is Great

Open any English version of the Bible and you will discover the heading "Great Commission" inserted somewhere in Matthew 28. Some Bibles have it before the first verse. Others put it ahead of verses 16 or 18. All have the phrase somewhere, even though it is clear that the heading was never part of the original text. Centuries after Matthew penned his Gospel, Bible translators inserted it into the body of text to guide readers into understanding the far-reaching implications of this passage.

In this instance, the adjective *great* is an appropriate modifier of commission." Of all the commissions found in Scripture, none compare to the greatness of this one. None are as far-reaching in authority, task, scope, strategy, and promise as this. What's more, obedience to this commission through the centuries has caused devout followers of Christ to expend an extraordinary amount of time, resources, prayer, sacrifice, and effort. Truly, it shows itself to be "great" in many respects.

Great in Authority

It is a common mistake for some to think that this commission begins with verse 19. That seems to be where most people begin when they quote it. But by beginning there, it cuts out one of the most important assurances Jesus could pass along to his disciples and those who would follow after them. In verse 18, he begins the commission by saying, "All authority in heaven and on earth has been given to me."

The commission is great in authority. Authority is different than power. One can wield a lot of power, yet not have proper authority to do so. I have three grown sons, and when they were younger each could not wait for the day that they could out-wrestle Dad. Over time, as their bodies developed into teenagers, they finally could take down and even pin Dad. Each one was elated when he could finally exercise power over me—the one who had exercised power over them all their lives! As a face-saving measure, however, as I slowly pulled myself off the floor, I would remind each of them that although he could now exert more power, I still had ultimate authority. I still made the rules of the house. I could still tell them what to do, what not to do, and when to do certain things. Though no longer stronger, I still had ultimate control through my authority as their father.

The propagation of the good news of Jesus Christ is God's sanctioned plan for this era in human history, and he stands behind it.

Jesus would remind his disciples of the power available to them during his final meeting with them, recorded in Acts 1. For now, he needs them to understand that his absolute, all-inclusive authority was the underpinning for reaching lost people. The right for them to go on mission anywhere, enter any country, encounter any culture, or witness in any community to persuade any person to believe in him was a God-given right, based on his authority. Therefore, that right was indisputable. It was this authority that gave Peter the boldness, when questioned about his witness, to say to the Jewish religious leaders, "We must obey God rather than men" (Acts 5:29). What audacity! But Peter's audacity was based on the divine authority he had received from Jesus.

That the mandate has its origin in God, whose sovereign rule is over all creation, is significant to the Great Commission. It is significant because it precludes that no man anywhere, no matter what his position of authority, can ever rightfully claim that the mission of the church is invalid or unjustified. No church anywhere can claim exemption from it, and no government of any country at any time can justify suppressing it. The mission given to the church is irrevocable and unstoppable.

The propagation of the good news of Jesus Christ is God's sanctioned plan for this era in human history, and he stands behind it. This realization that God's authority transcends all others' authority and underpins the efforts of those who go on mission has four practical implications.

For the missionary
God's message-bearer has the ongoing confidence that what he/she is doing is authorized by God and not based on his/her own will, inclination, plan, or impulse. His/Her calling is officially sanctioned, not done on his/her own initiative.

For the sending church
The sending church can know with certainty that its mission to the world is totally worthwhile and worthy of its efforts and resources (personnel, prayer, projects, money).

For the receiving church
Receiving churches, wherever they are found (including here in North America), need to recognize that foreign assistance from fellow believers is to be welcomed and utilized as it advances toward maturity, autonomy, and capability to also reach out. Outside assistance is to be accepted, not on the basis of availability nor because it is charitable, but because the provision has been authorized by God himself.

For governments
No matter the country or leader, those placed in governmental authority need to recognize that the Christian mission is not a form of foreign imperialism, nor is it a meddling in their internal affairs. Nor are God's ambassadors who are in their country a guise for a foreign "spiritual ploy," menacingly disrupting local communities. Rather, gospel outreach is something that has been mandated from a higher authority than they themselves possess. Missionaries enter their countries on no lesser a basis than on the authority of Almighty God, who has sent them there.

In this regard, Herbert Kane says it like no other.

The Great Commission then, is based on the supremacy and sovereignty of Jesus Christ, the Son of God, who in the Incarnation became the Son of Man, that through His death and resurrection He might become the Savior and Sovereign of the world. He is not only the Head of the church and the Lord of the harvest; He is also the Lord of history, the King of the nations, and the Arbiter of human destiny. Sooner or later all men must come to terms with Him. He and He alone has the right to demand universal allegiance."[34]

Great in Methodology

Jesus next tells his disciples what the specific method of his mission is to be followed:

Go therefore and make disciples of all nations, baptizing them in the name of the Father and of the Son and of the Holy Spirit, teaching them to observe all that I have commanded you. (Matthew 28:19-20)

If there is a focal point to the Great Commission, this is it. In the previous chapter I noted that evangelism is the highest priority of Jesus' mission. Now Jesus tells what specific outcome evangelism is to have: making disciples. Jesus specified what that means and how it is to be done.

An examination of the grammar shows that this sentence consists of four verbs. It consists of an imperative tied to three accompanying participles with modal force. The principle verb of the sentence is not the first one—*go*—but rather the second one—*make disciples*. The centerpiece of Jesus' command is the making of disciples.[35] Perhaps the intent of the sentence becomes clearer in this diagram:[36]

34 J. Herbert Kane, *Christian Missions in Biblical Perspective*, 149.
35 Terry, Smith, Anderson, *Missiology*, 71–72.
36 Adapted from Craig Blomberg, *A Survey of the Life of Christ*, 357.

"Make disciples"

Robert Coleman has stated, "The ultimate goal of Jesus for his disciples was that his life be reproduced through them into the lives of others."[37] The making of disciples is more than just the making of converts. Evangelism is not complete when a person gives a simple assent to the gospel message. The raising of a hand, the walking of an aisle, an uttering of a sinner's prayer, is not the culmination of the church's task. It is only the beginning.

> The command has been to "go," but we have stayed—in body, gifts, prayer and influence. He has asked us to be witnesses unto the uttermost parts of the earth ... but 99% of Christians have kept puttering around in the homeland.
> —Robert Savage

Granted, the good news is shared, and it is believed; but the mission doesn't stop there. Evangelism initiates the process of a person becoming a consistent follower of the Savior in whom they now believe. But this is not the making of disciples, or "discipleship," as some put it.

George Barna offers a succinct definition of a disciple as one who is "becoming a complete and competent follower of Jesus Christ."[38] Discipleship, then, is the process in which mature believers build personal relationships with new believers for the purpose of producing growing and competent followers of Jesus Christ. The process develops over a period of time and demands the building of relationship.

Producing authentic followers of Jesus is the goal of making disciples. These individuals evidence their genuineness in the faith by their progress in spiritual maturity that transforms their beliefs and behavior. Thus, I suggest an appropriate definition of a disciple to be:

> *a consistent follower of Christ, whose life is progressively being transformed into the image of Christ. This follower joyfully walks with Christ and is constantly being informed by Scripture, prayer, the Holy Spirit, and other believers, with the chief end of glorifying God.*

---

37 Robert E. Coleman, *The Master Plan of Evangelism*, 173.
38 George Barna, *Growing True Disciples* (Colorado Springs: Waterbook Press, 2001).

I like the way George Peters describes discipleship:

Discipleship is a path rather than an achievement. While there is growth and grading among the disciples, there are no graduated disciples. Discipleship is a perpetual school which may lead from one degree to another but does not graduate its scholars.[39]

Jesus' disciples understood firsthand what this discipleship process entailed. For the past three years, Jesus had lived with them, walked with them, and shared with them. They followed after him and fellowshipped with him, as everyday experiences became lessons on loving God, loving others, and denying self. Thus, they would have intuitively understood that all he had modeled to them, they were to likewise model for others.

Jesus goes on to tell the disciples that making other disciples is a three-step process: first, by going to those who had had no exposure to the gospel; second, by calling them into a relationship with Jesus that culminates in baptism; and third, by teaching them to observe his commands.[40]

"Go" (reaching out, or penetration)

The first step in making disciples is to go to where there are people who are not Christ-followers. Being placed first in the sentence shows that it is the first step; and actually, since it is linked with "make disciples," it carries a mild imperative force.[41] This is the third time the disciples heard they were to go somewhere. It shows the duty of believers to take the gospel from where it is known and believed to where it is not known and believed.

The verb can readily be translated "as you go," indicating concomitant circumstance. This is a reminder that in every experience of life, all believers should be sensitive to the presence of others around them who are in need of the gospel.[42]

"Baptizing them" (bringing in, or consolidation)

Jesus doesn't mean to use baptism as a magical rite that automatically brings people into relationship with Jesus without a change of heart. Sadly, it has deteriorated into that very thing in some church traditions. Rather, baptism is the culmination of the repent-believe-baptize experience of salvation.

---

39 George Peters, *A Biblical Theology of Missions*, 189.
40 Terry, Smith, Anderson, *Missiology*, 72.
41 Craig Blomberg, *Survey of the Life*, 356.
42 Terry, Smith, Anderson, *Missiology*, 73.

This public symbol of initiation is very meaningful. It is a picture of beginning a new life in Christ and of allegiance to him and to his church. The ordinance is a powerful outward expression of a new identity and a changed life within. Indeed, because of these implications, there are new believers in some hostile cultures who delay its application for fear of repercussion. Antagonistic nonbelievers understand its significance!

That believers are to be baptized in the name of the Father, Son, and Holy Spirit indicates the believer's new relationship with the triune God. The names of the three persons of the Trinity are invoked in baptism to show the significance of all three in the salvation experience. God the Father is the author of grace, Jesus is the provider of grace, and the Holy Spirit is the applicator of grace. The three work together in harmony to bring lost souls to the place of redemption. This Christian rite rightfully recognizes all three persons of the Godhead and teaches the new believer that this is the God who now is to be worshipped. Baptism, then, pictures all that is implied when a person repents of sin, believes in Christ, and is placed into the fellowship of believers.

"Teaching them" (changing over, or transformation)

The making of disciples does not stop with the initiation experience. There is an educational process that follows to keep new followers learning and growing in their new faith. Some today would equate this

> New believers are taught with the goal that they will become obedient followers of all Christ commanded.

with "spiritual formation." Whatever the label, the important thing is that there is an ongoing growth experience. The new believers' worldview must be changed, their lifestyle adjusted to increasingly conform to the image of Christ, and their ethical conduct increasingly marked by integrity. When transformation is apparent in these areas, the new believers in turn are in a position to teach others also and thus duplicate the process.

Teaching has a final goal—obedience. New believers are taught with the goal that they will become obedient followers of all Christ commanded. Among other things that Jesus taught, they are to live out the great commandment (Matt 22:37–40) and show great compassion (Matt 9:36). It takes growth experiences in community with other believers for this to be most effective. This is why believers are congregated into churches (and why some have labeled this passage in Matthew 28 the "church planting commission"). This is why missionaries have established Bible schools and seminaries the world over. This is why seminars, webinars, church-based training, and a host of other teaching ministries are so important. Growth happens best in the presence of other believers. It is the local church that best facilitates the fellowship of believers. "Iron sharpens iron, and one man sharpens another" (Prov 27:17). Thus, by implication, the establishment of local congregations is an outcome of the methodology for mission.[43] It is the best method to keep a disciple-making movement going within a community.

Superficial or genuine outcomes?

Thus, all three activities—going (penetration), baptizing (consolidation), and teaching (transformation)—are necessary components to discipleship. When done correctly, lives are genuinely changed. This is the ultimate objective of making disciples: the transformation of lives.

However, the lack of genuinely changed lives has turned out to be the greatest omission the world over when attempting to reach the unreached. All too often "proselytes" are made instead of "disciples." When this happens, churches get filled with bodies who exhibit little evidence of changed beliefs, worldviews, and behaviors. This results in either counterfeit cults or spiritually apathetic adherents who quickly deteriorate into nominal Christians. And nominal Christians, although they wear the tag "Christian," are not Christ-followers at all. They are superficial followers of "the way" in need of a conversion experience.

This sad state has become the bane of the church the world over. It causes skepticism when it comes to the validity of certain church planters' reports. Although it is common to read reports about myriads of conversions and prolific church planting movements, what is the value of those reports if they do not evidence the bearing of the fruit of transformed lives? Superficial conversions and inflated statistics only promote inauthentic outcomes.

It is incumbent on God's messengers to engage in a process of making disciples that has the transformation of lives as the final goal. Only then are people genuinely disciples of Christ. Only then is the intended outcome of Jesus' commission achieved among "all nations."

---

43 Senior and Stuhlmueller observe (p. 252), "Missionary proclamation includes the formation of a community, or 'church.' This is the implication of Matthew's use of the baptismal formula in 28:19. Such ecclesiastical interest harmonizes with the whole tone of Matthew's gospel. The *ekklesia* (or 'church') that gathers in Jesus' name (cf. 16:18, 18:17,20) is the place where the values of the kingdom are to be manifested: mercy, compassion, reconciliation."

Great in Scope

Speaking of all nations, what specifically did Jesus mean? The immediate response would indicate that Jesus seems to be speaking of the geopolitical "nations" wherein mankind dwells. At present, according to the United Nations count, there are 195 "nations" on our globe.[44] Is this what Jesus meant by reaching the nations? If so, it could be argued that a good share of people have been reached in every nation, and thus the reaching of the unreached is nearly complete.

But the phase *panta ta ethne* is a more technical phrase (*panta* = all, *ta* = the, *ethne* = nations) with a more precise meaning. One of the first encounters of this phrase is in Genesis 12:3. The Greek Septuagint translation of that Hebrew phrase is the same as is found here in Matthew 28: Abraham was to be a blessing to *panta ta ethne* ("all the nations"). The blessing from Abraham would reach into every ethno-linguistic group on earth. Of course, this could only happen through a distant descendant of Abraham—namely, Jesus—who would be the blessing to the entire world (Gal 3:14).

The phrase is used various other places in the New Testament, including the Luke commission passage (Luke 24:47). In the book of Revelation, the phrase takes on a clearer definition as two visions of the future makeup of peoples around the throne of God are portrayed by John.

Revelation 5:9 and 7:9 assume the central missionary task of reaching people groups has taken place by the end times. The use and order of the specific terms in the two passages are compared as follows:

Revelation 5:9	Revelation 7:9
Tribe	*Nation*
Language	*Tribe*
People	*People*
Nation	*Language*

Although the word order is different, these nouns describing people groups are identical. These verses not only refer to the universality of the spreading of the gospel, but also to the depth in societies where the gospel will reach.

---

44 There are 195 countries in the world today. This total comprises 193 countries that are member states of the United Nations and two countries that are non-member observer states: the Holy See and the State of Palestine. https://www.worldometers.info/geography/how-many-countries-are-there-in-the-world/.

One last heavenly vision is found in Revelation 15:2–4. This "song of Moses" and "song of the Lamb" is the great doxology sung by the myriads who come out of the tribulation period victorious. The words of this song are significant in relation to the extent of world evangelization. Victorious peoples praise God by singing,

> Great and marvelous are your deeds, Lord God Almighty.
> Just and true are your ways, King of the nations.
> Who will not fear you, Lord,
>   and bring glory to your name?
> For you alone are holy,
> All nations (panta ta ethne) will come and worship before you,
>   for your righteous acts have been revealed. —Revelation 15:3–4 NIV

In chapter 1, I mentioned that the world contains 17,468 ethnically distinct people groups. Of these, 7,419 (or 41.8 percent) are classified as unreached. These unreached people groups contain 3.2 billion of the 7.8 billion people living in the world today–well over A Third of Us!

The scope of Jesus' mission is vast. He is telling his church that the evangelistic task should not be considered complete until there will be a representative from every ethno-linguistic group on earth praising God in heaven.

Great in Promise

Jesus closes his instruction with the most tender of assurances, meant to encourage the hearts of those who would launch out to reach the still unreached. He leaves the disciples with the promise that he will always be with them as they spread the good news far and wide. This can be called "the comforting clause" of the Great Commission, as those words were intended to do just that—bring comfort and assurance to any who engage in global outreach. Jesus promises,

> "And behold, I am with you always, to the end of the age."

Jesus knew that in a few short weeks he would be leaving the disciples permanently. But because of his abiding spiritual presence with them after his ascension, he promises to go with each of the Eleven as they in turn go on their various mission outreaches.

Although the impact of this promise was not realized at the moment, what a comfort it must have been to the disciples as they later fanned out across the globe. That same promise still gives comfort and assurance to Christ's ambassadors today as they forsake all and leave their homelands for the sake of the gospel.

Although "end of the age" has been translated "end of the world" in some translations, this temporal rendering is more accurate than a geographical one. It is the same word from which we get our word *eons*. Though this may be a technical point, it is reassuring to know that even more than at any place, Jesus is with his messengers at all times in every age. His ongoing presence is promised right through to the end of this age. There is no place they go where he will not be present and no time when he will be absent. The omnipresent and eternal nature of Jesus guarantees this promise always to be true.

Probably no other prayer says it better than the one attributed to the famous medieval Celtic missionary, Patrick. Read closely the words of confidence from a segment of the poem, "The Breastplate of St. Patrick":

I arise today, through God's strength to pilot me: God's might to uphold me, God's wisdom to guide me, God's eye to look before me, God's ear to hear me, God's word to speak for me, God's hand to guard me, God's way to lie before me, God's shield to protect me, God's host to secure me: against snares of devils, against temptations of vices, against inclinations of nature, against everyone who shall wish me ill, afar and near, alone and in a crowd.

I summon today all these powers between me (and these evils): against every cruel and merciless power that may oppose my body and my soul: against incantations of false prophets, against black laws of heathenry, against false laws of heretics, against craft of idolatry, against spells of women [any witch] and smiths and wizards, against every knowledge that endangers man's body and soul. Christ to protect me today: against poison, against burning, against drowning, against wounding, so that there may come abundance of reward.

Christ with me, Christ before me, Christ behind me, Christ in me, Christ beneath me, Christ above me, Christ on my right, Christ on my left, Christ in breadth, Christ in length, Christ in height, Christ in the heart of every man who thinks of me, Christ in the mouth of every man who speaks of me, Christ in every eye that sees me, Christ in every ear that hears me.

57

*I arise today through a mighty strength,
the invocation of the Trinity, through
belief in the Three-ness, through
confession of the Oneness of the
Creator of creation. Salvation is of
the Lord. Salvation is of the Lord.
Salvation is of Christ. May Thy
Salvation, O Lord, be ever with us.*[45]

Charles Spurgeon summed up the teaching of this commission of Matthew 28 with the following:

This is the perpetual commission of the Church of Christ; and the great seal of the Kingdom attached to it, giving the power to execute it, and guaranteeing its success, is the King's assurance of his continued presence with his faithful followers.[46]

45 "The Breast-plate of St. Patrick," *The Season* website, http://www.theseason.org/breast.htm.
46 Charles Spurgeon, *The Gospel of Matthew*, 416.

REACHING A THIRD OF US

Jesus did not want his followers to be timid in spreading the good news of his redemption to the world. Rather, he wanted them to give a bold witness, and he assured them that they had the authority to go anywhere at any time based on the fact that the mandate had been authorized by Jesus himself.

As they went, their evangelistic efforts were to culminate in the making of disciples—i.e., consistent followers of Jesus whose lives are increasingly being transformed into the image of Christ. New followers were to be baptized and taught to observe Christ's commands and demands on their lives in the context of Christian community—the church.

The task should never be considered completed until there are thriving believers found in every ethno-linguistic group on earth. This means going beyond the geo-political borders by which human beings have divided themselves, right into the heart of every ethnic group found within those borders.

As they go, Christ's messengers need not feel they are doing this task alone. Jesus' comforting presence will be with them at all times, right up to the end of this age. There is no place they can go where he will not be present, no time when he will be absent. The omnipresent and eternal nature of Jesus guarantees this promise to be true.

CHAPTER 6

The Message We Share Luke 24:44–49

"Like cold water to a thirsty soul, so is good news from a far country." —King Solomon; Proverbs 25:25

"The gospel is not how people get to heaven; the gospel is how people get to God." —John Piper

J ust what message do we proclaim to the unreached? That's a very important question. The good news we share needs to be true, precise, and meaningful if it is to get any kind of a hearing by those hearing it for the first time. We who proclaim it need to take care that it aligns with God's eternal plan of redemption, a cosmic drama being played out, beginning with the book of Genesis. That is why this passage from the Gospel of Luke is important. The instructions of Jesus recorded here tell us precisely what the essence of the message is that we are to convey to the unreached.

Beginning with the evening of Resurrection Day, Jesus had met off and on with his disciples at various locations over a forty-day period. He had two primary objectives for those meetings: 1) to convince them by way of many irrefutable proofs that he was indeed alive and had experienced a bodily resurrection (Acts 1:3); and 2) to prepare them for their next assignment. They were close to graduating from being followers (disciples) to becoming global ambassadors (apostles). As apostles, they were to become the pioneer bearers of the good news.

Thus, at this meeting recorded by Luke, Jesus' goal is to explain the message they were to bear as they went to the unreached. The value of his redemptive work, and its becoming known to all mankind, depended upon them being convinced about it themselves. Jesus wanted them to get it right.

The Three "P's" of Evangelism

Before we look at the message itself, it is helpful to review what it means to evangelize. I mentioned earlier that evangelization can be relegated to three components: presence, proclamation, and persuasion. The example of a believer exhibiting a moral, Christ-centered life (presence), coupled with a verbal witness (proclamation), culminating in urging others to appropriate for themselves Christ's work of grace (persuasion), encompasses evangelism.

The information Jesus has passed along to his disciples up to this point comprises the core of evangelism. Notice the three "P's" of evangelism embedded in the Great Commission passages that Jesus had initiated so far:

"As you go" (Matthew 28:19)

World Presence ⇨	Proclamation ⇨	Persuasion = Evangelization
"So send I you" (John 20:21)	"Preach the gospel" (Mark 16:15)	"Make disciples" (Matthew 28:18–20)

Jesus knew that the activity of evangelization in and of itself, although important, was not sufficient. It needed substance. It needed to be connected to a relevant message that met a dire need of the hearers. He also knew that the importance of that message needed to be clearly understood if the disciples were to devote the rest of their lives to proclaiming it. Therefore, his intent at this fourth encounter was to ground them in the essence of the message they were going to proclaim.

The Need for the Message

When you stop and think about it, ambassadors of the gospel in all ages have had a lot of audacity. They have had the audacity to leave their homeland to live cross-culturally in other countries and cultures. They have had the audacity to proclaim a strange message to the peoples of that culture. They also have had the audacity to challenge followers of other belief systems to abandon their long-held beliefs and embrace a new set of convictions. This new message many times is as foreign to the hearer as the person who brings it to them.

The gospel is rarely automatically believed when heard for the first time. One mitigating reason is that the worldview of a culture is informed by the belief system that has become the warp and woof of

Men are in this plight not because they are unevangelized, but because they are men. Sin is the destroyer of the soul and the destruction of the knowledge of God which is life. And it is not the failure to have heard the gospel which makes men sinners. The gospel would save them if they heard it and accepted it, but it is not the ignorance or rejection of the gospel which destroys them, it is the knowledge of sin.
—Robert E. Speer

63

that society for generations. Another factor is that the meaning of a message across cultures many times gets distorted in its transmission, causing the message, at least at first, to become incomprehensible.[47] But these factors aside, the deeper reason for nonacceptance of the gospel is the societal concept of mankind's spiritual root problem or predicament. The belief of man's root problem varies from ethnic group to ethnic group. It is inescapably linked to the belief system that undergirds a society. A quick survey of the belief systems of unreached people bears this out.

Animism

Over two hundred and thirty-two million of the earth's inhabitants are animists.[48] Animistic peoples consider unseen spirits that permeate the world around them as the culprits for their spiritual and physical plight. Their worst nightmare is to have a spirit or band of spirits antagonize them or bring them harm. Their energies are focused on appeasing the spirit world through ritualistic practices. Since there is no high god to assist them, they must help themselves by manipulating the spirit world as best they can. As such, this is a religion of practical humanism.

Hinduism

Hindus view their spiritual predicament a little differently. Although spirits need to be contended with, for them ignorance is the greater cause of deep-seated human problems. If they only were better enlightened, they would know how to be delivered from their problems. Therefore, better knowledge, combined with the ritualistic appeasement of multiple gods and spirits, delivers them out of their nagging spiritual predicament.

Buddhism

Buddhists take this matter a step farther. For them, suffering is the greatest human predicament, and the primary cause of suffering is human desire. Unchecked desires cause the greatest of problems and the deepest of sufferings. Therefore, following Buddha's four noble truths that extend into his eight-fold path will bring control to human desire.

---

47 Eugene Nida deals extensively with this topic in *Meaning Across Culture*. Although an older anthropological work, Nida's observations about meaning in culture still hold true today.

48 Animists believe that the world around them is pulsating with unseen menacing spirits. These spirits need to be appeased if they are not to cause harm, injury, or even death. Although tribal peoples are most steeped in these beliefs, elements of animism are found in all of the major world religions to one degree or another. New Age channelers and spiritists hold to the identical basic beliefs.

Islam

On the other hand, Muslims believe selfishness to be at the core of man's predicament. Allah's wrath falls on those who, out of selfishness, refuse to submit to him. This is manifested by wrongdoing on man's part. Therefore, one needs to work feverishly to rid oneself of the weight of those wrong deeds. By so doing, Allah will be appeased. The way to do that is by submitting to him (the word *Muslim* means "one who is submitted") through constant engagement in five fundamentals, or "pillars," of belief and practice. On the merits of consistent engagement in these fundamentals, a person can save himself. This makes Islam the most autosoteric, or self-saving, religion among all religions.

Judaism

Finally, the modern-day Jew has his own idea of his predicament. Jews are found grouped into a variety of branches that hold to various levels of orthodoxy. A common thread that runs through this religion is the belief that broken relationships are the root cause of one's deepest problems.[49] It is therefore incumbent upon the Jew to mend broken relationships and maintain good ones at all costs. Relationships of most concern are those between family members, within communities, between adherents of other religions, and with God.

All of these beliefs have something in common with Christianity. They all focus on an aspect of life that is of deepest concern to every human—man's spiritual plight. However, that is where the similarity stops. As widespread as the representation of predicaments found among them is, none go far enough in pinpointing man's true root problem, as revealed in Scripture.

To use a medical metaphor, each religion, in its own way, focuses on a symptom of man's deepest problem, but not on the disease itself. In other words, each religion's adherents concern themselves with external circumstances that they attempt to control through rituals and religious practices. Sadly, all fall short of what Scripture pinpoints as man's real root problem—sin.

As I write this, the coronavirus is running rampant throughout the world. It manifests itself in various symptoms: headaches, vomiting, high temperature, shortness of breath, chills, confusion, etc. The real culprit,

---

49 Winfried Corduan, *Neighboring Faiths*, 45–46.

though, is the virus itself, not the symptoms. A cure is needed for the virus, not the symptoms. The same is true when it comes to sin. The need is for message-bearers to proclaim a lucid message about the problem of sin. Jesus knew this and used this encounter in Luke 24 to teach the disciples the essence of the message that we are to proclaim.

The Content of the Message

Jesus knew that his good-news message would be as applicable to the pluralistic environment of the twenty-first century as it was to that of the first, and to every century in between. He also knew that in its simplest form it need not be theologically complicated. He understood how words of help and hope would resonate with human needs, no matter the culture the listeners are a part of or the worldview to which they adhere.

Therefore, at this fourth post-resurrection encounter, Jesus told the disciples to proclaim a message that was succinct yet meaningful to any person living anywhere in any culture. Its relevancy to anyone and everyone was not to be lost on the disciples. All that a person needs to know is encompassed in one sentence. Jesus opened their minds to understand the Old Testament Scriptures, and said to them, "Thus it is written, that the Christ should suffer and on the third day rise from the dead, and that repentance for the forgiveness of sins should be proclaimed in his name to all nations, beginning from Jerusalem" (Luke 24:46–47).

In brief, Jesus made four vital statements that comprise the essence of the gospel:

1. Who Jesus is: the promised Messiah (Christ)
2. What Jesus did: suffered, died, and rose from the dead
3. How one is to respond: repentance
4. What benefit is gained: forgiveness of sins

Put another way, the gospel includes three essential truths:

1. The reality of sin as man's greatest predicament.
2. The redemptive work of Jesus as the only cure for that predicament.
3. The response of repentance that is necessary for a sinner to be forgiven of sins.

These three truths encompass the essence of the gospel. This is all a person needs to know and believe to experience a right relationship with God. This is all that is necessary to have a salvation experience.

The Message Expanded

As concise as the gospel message is, Jesus took the opportunity to expound on that information. By doing so, he was both laying the underpinning of the message and assuring its propagation to all peoples.

These three truths encompass the essence of the gospel. This is all a person needs to know and believe to experience a right relationship with God.

1. The basis of the message: Old Testament Scripture

"Thus it is written." The gospel has never been a stand-alone message that was concocted either by Jesus or his disciples. It is a message rooted in the Old Testament Jewish Scriptures. The story of redemption began in Genesis, was developed throughout the Old Testament, and then found its fulfillment in Jesus—the promised Messiah. It is a message reinforced by Old Testament imagery and prophecy. Jesus' sacrificial death for sin was the apex of God's redemptive plan, which had been initiated centuries earlier.

2. The core of the message: Christ suffered, died, and rose from the dead

Part 1: Christ suffered and died

> *There was only one way that the totality of God's holiness and justice could be met and satisfied. Only through the uniqueness of Christ's sinless personhood and atoning work could that be done. Only the one and only perfect Son of God dying for sin once for all could do that. In his death Jesus paid the price for sin, freeing God up to offer forgiveness to sinful man (2 Cor 5:21). Paul states it this way: "In Christ God was reconciling the world to himself" (2 Cor 5:19). In Christ's suffering, all the requirements of God's holiness, justice, love, and mercy were met (Rom 3:25–26).*

Part 2: Christ rose from the dead

> *The resurrection of Christ from the dead proved that he was divine and the sole provider of salvation. This is the centerpiece of the Christian message: the bodily resurrection of the historical Christ. The validity of the entire gospel story rests on the reality of Jesus' bodily resurrection.*

For the apostles who saw and fellowshipped with Jesus after his resurrection, this became the bedrock of the gospel. All the Gospel writers conclude their accounts of the life of Christ with an account of his resurrection from the dead. This reality became the dominant theme of all preaching and teaching in the infant church. This reality was woven into all gospel presentations in the book of Acts (1:2, 25; 2:22–36; 3:15; 4:10, 33; 5:30; 7:56; 9:4; 10:40; 13:30–37; 17:3, 31–32; 22:7; 26:14).[50]

3. The requirement of the message: Repentance

The repentance (*metanoian*) that is to be proclaimed carries a specific meaning. It is used to denote the need to "have another mind" by changing one's opinion about something.

> True repentance has intellectual, emotional and volitional elements. Intellectually, it involves a change of mind about God, sin, Christ and oneself. The resultant change of mind views God as good and holy; sin as evil and injurious before God and people; Christ as perfect, necessary, and sufficient for salvation; and oneself as guilty and in need of salvation. Such repentance is an essential element of missionary proclamation.[51]

Though repentance is necessary for salvation, it is not meritorious in and of itself. Christ's death is what fully satisfied God's requirement for righteousness (Rom 3:25). Repentance is the nonnegotiable response to the gospel message.

4. The provision of the message: Forgiveness of sins

The Christian message is a glorious message of pardon. God has granted full pardon from man's nemesis—namely, sin. When we repent, we are freed from the penalty of sin, the power of sin, and—in future glory—from the presence of sin. The extent of forgiveness is total and eternal! It takes care of a person's past, present, and future. What can be better than that?!

The Greek word here, *aphesis*, translated as "forgiveness," carries the idea of dismissal, or release. It is intended to show a deliverance, or liberty, that comes through a legal pardon. God suspends, or "sends away," for all eternity the just penalty of sin on behalf of the repentant sinner.[52] The punishment due mankind was paid for by Jesus (Rom 5:6–10; Eph 2:13).

Thus, forgiveness of sins is at the very heart of the Christian message. There is no other message like it anywhere in the world. No other religion promises full pardon, either in this life or the next. No other religion completely cures man's spiritual predicament. No other religion can say with

50 Harold Dollar, "Resurrection of Christ," *Evangelical Dictionary of World Missions*, 827.
51 Bill Thrasher, "Repentance," *Evangelical Dictionary of World Missions*, 824.
52 W. E. Vine, An *Expository Dictionary of New Testament Words*, 122–23.

confidence, "There is therefore now no condemnation for those who are in Christ Jesus" (Rom 8:1).

5. The necessity of the message: Sin as man's spiritual predicament

The sin nature found within every human being is the root spiritual predicament of all mankind. There are no exceptions.

The sin nature found within every human being is the root spiritual predicament of all mankind. There are no exceptions. The Scriptures tell us that man is sinful by nature, by birth, and by choice.[53] Sin is more than moral failure on man's part. It is "missing the mark" of God's righteousness altogether. It entails rebellion against the very person of God.

Sin is so deeply ingrained in the human soul that none of us have the ability to rectify the problem in and of ourselves. Sin's roots penetrate so deep into the human heart that its ugly head keeps appearing and reappearing no matter how hard people try to beat it back. Because of this predicament, human beings forever manifest their sinfulness through ignorance, desire, wrongdoing, broken relationships, and fear of spirits.

What's more, we fail miserably in our attempt to conquer these and other selfish manifestations. That is why Jesus came to the rescue. That is why he wants his message of rescue known. That is why our message is so important. That is why Jesus could so confidently say to the disciples on the evening of his betrayal that he alone is "the way, and the truth, and the life" (John 14:6).

This leads us back to the world religions and their various notions about man's predicament. They also have various responses about what can be done.

The animist is basically clueless and would ask, "What way? What truth? What life?"

The Hindu would say, "Discover a way, discover a truth, discover a life" among the pantheon of gods that permeate their religion.

The Buddhist would suggest that one "follow a way, follow a truth, and follow a life" as prescribed by the Buddha.

---

53 As SEND International's unpublished paper, "Salvation of the Unevangelized," asserts, "The clear statements of Scripture teach that all men are sinners by nature, choice and practice (Rom 3:9–19; 5:12). All people are under God's wrath and judgment because their sin is an affront to God's perfect holiness (Rom 1:18; 2:5–6; 1 Pet. 1:16). All people deserve the judgment of God because of their inherited and willful sin (Rom 6:23)." (IC '96/SEND International)

Notice that each of these religions prescribe a path of self-deliverance based on meritorious works.

The Muslim would say that a person is to "submit to a way, submit to a truth, and submit to a life" as dictated by the prophet Mohammad through the Koran and Sharia law.

Finally, the Jew would say that we are to "build a way, build a truth, and build a life" that promotes wholesomeness across the broad spectrum of human relationships.

Notice that each of these religions prescribe a path of self-deliverance based on meritorious works. But none of them get to the root problem of the human heart. Only Jesus provides both the answer and the provision to man's spiritual predicament. That is why Jesus could boldly say that he alone is the *way* out of sin, that he alone possesses the *truth* about sin, and that he alone provides a *life* free from the penalty of sin. Jesus alone fully and eternally takes care of man's sin problem.

6. The extension of the message: To all nations

Here Jesus uses the same phrase that he did during his previous encounter with the disciples, recorded in Matthew 28. Jesus attaches "beginning from Jerusalem" to the phrase "to all nations" (*panta ta* ethne; discussed in the previous chapter) to show the extent of where the gospel is to be carried, along with from where it was to start out.

The disciples were no doubt tempted to return to their home area of Galilee and begin their mission from there. That would have been the natural thing to do. Jesus knew that if they did return home, they might never have gone out to reach the unreached. Back with family and friends and fishing gear, it would have been very tempting for them not to go to any nations at all.

The mission had to begin in Jerusalem. There were clear advantages as to why it needed to begin there. One advantage was to reach as many Jews as possible from all over the empire. Many Jews from all over would be converging on Jerusalem in a few days to celebrate the feast of Pentecost. Many would hear and believe the message Peter preached in Acts 2. Those who responded would then jump-start the spread of the gospel to all nations when they returned home as new Christ-followers.

Another reason for the disciples to stay in Jerusalem was so they would have maximum impact on the center of Judaism. This is where the truth of the gospel had a chance to be encountered by the most important and astute of the religious leaders. Jesus foresaw that many of these influential leaders would themselves embrace the message (Acts 6:7).

But probably the most important reason to stay in Jerusalem was because that would be the place where the Holy Spirit would corporately fall upon them. The empowerment needed for the task would come through this "other Comforter"—the other person of the Triune God. Once the disciples experienced the Spirit's baptism, they would be free to proclaim the gospel as widely and as far as they wished.

Empowerment for the Task

Thus, once Jesus had briefed the disciples on the essence of the message, he told them not to go anywhere until they were first properly equipped:

> *Behold, I am sending the promise of my Father upon you. But stay in the city until you are clothed with power from on high. – Luke 24:49*

Jesus could not overemphasize the importance of this needed empowerment. He knew it was such a crucial means to world evangelization that he mentioned the enabling of the Holy Spirit three times in the five commissions. He hinted at it during the first meeting, on the evening of Resurrection Day, when he breathed on them and—speaking symbolically and prophetically—said to them, "Receive the Holy Spirit" (John 20:22). He mentioned the empowerment again here, using the symbolism of being "clothed" by the Holy Spirit (Luke 24:49). He will mention it one last time at his farewell address with them shortly thereafter (Acts 1:8).

Today, just as in those days, the task of reaching the lost—especially cross-culturally—can only be carried out effectively through the supernatural enablement of the Holy Spirit. Only the Spirit can empower and energize believers for the task that in every respect is far too daunting and dangerous for them to accomplish on their own. Upon hearing these words, the disciples probably called to mind the words of the prophet Zechariah to another person (Zerubbabel) who too had been given a commission: "Not by might, nor by power, but by my Spirit, says the LORD of hosts" (Zech 4:6).

REACHING A THIRD OF US

The message of redemption is vitally important. Every religion has its view of humankind's spiritual predicament, but they all fall short of nailing what the problem really is: man's sinfulness. Humanity's sinful offenses against God—by nature, by birth, and by choice—have resulted in alienation from God. That broken relationship can only be mended by belief in the redemptive work of Christ on our behalf.

This message of redemption is based on the Old Testament revelation of God. At its core is Christ's death and resurrection. All that we are left to do is to appropriate, by faith, Christ's work on our behalf. If we do, we will experience the forgiveness of our sins, solving our nagging spiritual predicament.

This message is for all peoples. For good reasons, it started by being propagated from Jerusalem after the disciples were empowered by the Holy Spirit. From there it fanned its way out to the nations, being disseminated far and wide, first by the apostles and then by those who came after them. This continues to be our task today.

CHAPTER 7

The Means of Reaching Acts 1:8

"We must not be contented however with praying, without exerting ourselves in the use of means for the obtaining of the things we pray for."   —William Carey

"The use of means ought not to lessen our faith in God; and our faith in God ought not to hinder our using whatever means He has given us for the accomplishment of His own purposes."   —J. Hudson Taylor

The time had finally arrived for Jesus to leave his disciples permanently. One last meeting was all he needed to give them his final instruction. Over the past forty days he had progressively led them into an understanding of what he was asking of them when it came to their mission to the unreached. Now, one last piece of information would complete all he needed them to know before they got started.

Jesus' farewell address recorded in Acts 1 is really a continuation of what he had given them earlier in the day in an upper room in Jerusalem (Luke 24). With that session completed, Jesus had them join him on a trek of a little more than half a mile outside the city to the Mount of Olives (Acts 1:12). After clarifying some teaching about the timing of the kingdom, his final words were brief:

> You will receive power when the Holy Spirit has come upon you, and you will be my witnesses in Jerusalem and in all Judea and Samaria, and to the end of the earth – Acts 1:8

That was it! With that he lifted into the air never to be seen or heard from again. No wonder they lingered, gazing intently upward until interrupted by "two men … in white robes" (Acts 1:10).

If those parting words had been stand-alone instructions unattached to the previous four commission statements, the disciples would have been left dumbfounded. Instead, since they had been recipients of a succession of instructions, they grasped what Jesus meant.

In this final instruction, Jesus relayed three means of how mission to the unreached was to be carried out: the means of empowerment, the means of a strategic plan, and the means of human instrumentality.

The Means of Empowerment

The Holy Spirit is the divine Empowerer. His coming imparted the divine enabling to every aspect of the mission enterprise. As Robert Glover has said, "Christian missions are no human undertaking, but a supernatural and divine enterprise for which God has provided supernatural power and leadership." [1]It is the tendency of the human heart to rely on its own self-confidence and abilities for success in ministry. We easily mislead ourselves into thinking that human achievement can bring about spiritual results. But Jesus knew otherwise. He knew the spiritual battle that would ensue with the propagation of the gospel story. He also knew that the apostles were in no way equal to the task without empowerment from on high. They would "not wrestle against flesh and blood, but against the rulers, against the authorities, against the cosmic powers over this present darkness, against the spiritual forces of evil in the heavenly places" (Eph 6:12). That is why Jesus told the disciples:

"You will receive power when the Holy Spirit has come upon you."

An important principle in missions is clear: Spiritual work takes spiritual power to achieve spiritual ends. In light of this principle, it is imperative that we, like the disciples, are assured of where the source of power for mission originates.

> Christians will faithfully fulfill their missionary calling only if they do God's mission in God's way. Such mission has its origin in God the Father. Jesus knows that if His disciples are ever going to faithfully carry out the demands of mission, they cannot depend merely on themselves.... We need the Holy Spirit. Our own personal resources are valuable, but they are not sufficient.
> —Neville Callam

What about Management and Technology?

In this highly pragmatic and secular-humanistic age, it is easy to rely on managerial missiology to achieve missional goals.[54] The mission endeavor often deteriorates into a solely human endeavor with superficial results. It becomes purely human achievement and humanistic when based on self-sufficiency. All too often organizational efficiency replaces spiritual efficacy, resulting in a flurry of activity lacking genuine results. Back in the 1970s, John Stott, cognizant of this propensity of the human heart, looked ahead to our present day and insightfully wrote:

> *Some people seem to look forward with relish to the time when the evangelistic work of the church will be computerized, the whole job will be done by machines instead of people, and the evangelization of the world will be the ultimate triumph of human technology.*[55]

54 Engle and Dyrness, *Changing the Mind of Missions*, 69. In this regard, Engel and Dyrness say, "... it quickly can lead to the seductive temptation to reduce world missions to a manageable enterprise—with a large hierarchical structure to carry it out. Samuel Escabar has coined the phrase 'managerial missiology' to refer to an unduly pragmatic endeavor to reduce reality to an understandable picture, and then to project missionary action as a response to a problem that has been described in quantitative form."

55 John Stott, *Christian Mission in the Modern World*, 125.

Stott was a prophet of the times! How often have we heard it said that now that we have mastered the internet, cable TV, computer programs, text messaging, and whatever else may come along, that we finally have the ability to evangelize the world. Granted, these technologies do assist in the task, but they can never replace the power of the Holy Spirit in world evangelization.

Power

Jesus had already assured the apostles about the authority they had been granted for mission (Matt 28:18). That overarching authority gave them the right to go anywhere and at any time to engage a lost world. Now he informs them of the power (*dunamis*) available to them through the presence of the Holy Spirit.

The disciples knew they would be at a disadvantage without Jesus physically present by their side. It was an assurance to them, therefore, to know that another divine member of the Trinity would be with them and do for them what they could not do in and of themselves. By his power they would have the courage both to preach the gospel effectively and to work miracles that would confirm the gospel message.

Holy Spirit Power

In the midst of the aforementioned modern climate of self-confidence built on technological achievement and corporate managerial acumen applied to missions, it is refreshing to hearken back to the disciples' humble reliance on the power of the Holy Spirit. They believed that human beings, being dead in the trespasses of sins, blinded to spiritual truth, and enslaved to unrighteousness, could never save themselves out of the clutches of Satan. They knew that only the Holy Spirit could liberate people from the bondage of sin, bringing them from death into life.[56] It could only be by the empowerment of the Holy Spirit that the task of taking redemption to a sin-infested world could be achieved. Like us, they needed that empowerment.

Throughout the book of Acts, the Holy Spirit's empowerment was repeatedly manifested in relation to the mission of the church. The Spirit was so intricately involved in empowering the apostles throughout every aspect of their journey to the unreached, that his presence cannot be missed. In Acts, we see the Holy Spirit explicitly mentioned in regard to empowering for …

---

56 Stott, *Christian Mission*, 125.

1. Clear public proclamation of the gospel (Peter, in 2:14–41)
2. Bold defense before authorities (Peter, in 4:8–22)
3. Directing them to prepared hearts (Philip meeting the Ethiopian official, in 8:26–40; Peter meeting Cornelius, in 10:19–21)
4. Selecting new missionaries (church of Antioch, in 13:1–4)
5. Confronting spiritual forces (Paul confronting Elymas, in 13:9–12)
6. Settling theological issues resulting from the advance of the gospel into Gentile territory (Jerusalem Council, in 15:23–29)
7. Directing the steps of missionaries: guidance as to where *not* to go (Paul, in 16:6); guidance as to where to go (Paul compelled by the Holy Spirit to go to Jerusalem, in 20:22)
8. Guiding in the selection of leaders for mission churches (20:28)
9. Insight concerning future experiences a missionary would encounter (Paul told in advance about being taken captive in Jerusalem, in 21:4–11).

Empowerment by the Holy Spirit is such a dominant theme in the book of Acts that some have proposed that a better title for the book would be "Acts of the Holy Spirit."[57] In the apostolic church, as it should be today, the power of the Holy Spirit in mission was at the center of every endeavor.

Reflecting on the importance of the Holy Spirit in missions, George Peters said it well:

> *It is clearly implied and understood from the context and the general tenor of the Bible that such a task can be carried through only in the power of the Holy Spirit. He is the great Superintendent, the Energizer and Sustainer of His church. The church's task, in the final end, is a supernatural task which demands supernatural resources. Because these are available in the Holy Spirit we must lean hard upon him.*[58]

---

57 John Stott, *Message of Acts*, 33. Stott himself was of the opinion that the title "Acts of the Holy Spirit" overemphasizes the divine and overlooks the apostles as the chief characters through whom the Spirit worked. His suggestion of a better title would be "The Continuing Words and Deeds of Jesus by his Spirit through the Apostles."

58 George Peters, *A Biblical Theology of Missions*, 214. Peters also added this important note: "Since the Christian life is charged with supernatural ideals and demands, it can only be believed in absolute reliance on the Holy Spirit. Unless the lessons are learned early, the Christian life becomes beset with frustrations and numbness; apathy sets in, or people become conditioned to an abnormal or subnormal Christian life. This is the tragedy of countless believers who do not even expect to live up to the biblical ideals" (213–14).

The Means of a Strategic Plan

The book of Acts is a historical record of the geographic, linguistic, and ethnic expansion of the gospel. Acts 1:8 doubles as a table of contents for the book. The gospel was first preached among the Jews of Jerusalem and Judea (Acts 1–8), and then to the mixed-Jews of Samaria (Acts 8–12), and finally to the Gentiles everywhere else (Acts 13–28). However, Jesus teaches other things about missions in Acts 1:8 as well.

No One Center

The nature of the global mission of the church demands that it should never establish one geographic center as an exclusive hub. Jesus, wanting to make sure the disciples did not establish Jerusalem as their center, explicitly told them to go out from that city. The Old Testament version of centripetal mission, where Israel welcomed all nations streaming to it, was to be replaced by the centrifugal mission of going out to the nations. Christianity was not to be an ethnically Jewish-centric religion, a linguistically Hebrew-centric religion, or a geographically Jerusalem-centric religion. The straitjacket of the culture of Judaism was not to be imposed upon Christianity.

As such, Christianity was not designed to be a Jewish *axis mundi* (center from which everything revolves) religion. Freedom from this concept would permit it to flourish in any location and in any culture. The notion of a holy, centralized center of religion was not to be part of this new faith.

The genius of Christianity is that God can genuinely be worshipped wherever believers are found, in ways that are culturally appropriate to them. The concept of Christianity being polycentric—having a multitude of centers throughout the world—would become the model that would permit this new belief to thrive.[59] The fact that Jerusalem initially did become the center of Christianity was to have a short lifespan by design. This may be an extenuating reason why God allowed the city's destruction in AD 70. There was to be no permanent center![60]

---

59 Lamin Sanneh, *Disciples of All Nations: Pillars of World Christianity*, 13–14. Sanneh adds, "As the ancient scribe foresaw, in the age of true religion God's name would no longer be confined to one place but would be known and honored everywhere among the Gentiles. The witness of believers that God was their only dwelling place has been validated."

60 As the events in the book of Acts unfold, Luke informs us of the springing up of regional centers of Christianity. Although Jerusalem held the distinction of being the sole center of the church for twenty years, by the middle of the book (by the AD 50s), Antioch is mentioned as a strong center. Toward the end of the book (AD 60s), Ephesus is a growing center of influence, with the hint of Rome emerging on the scene as an upcoming center.

Three Places at Once

Jesus also told the apostles that their witness would take place in three arenas simultaneously. They were to have a witness in their capital city, Jerusalem, and in the immediate environs of Judea, subsequently radiate to the half-breeds in Samaria, and then go far beyond Palestine to "the end of the earth."

Some assume that the spreading of the gospel was to be a three-step process: first to Jerusalem and Judea, then on to Samaria, and finally stretching to the end of the earth. But the language of the text, to the contrary, points to a simultaneous witness in all three areas at the same time. The verse literally reads:

> You will be my witnesses in Jerusalem *and* in all Judea *and* Samaria *and* to the end of the earth.

The *ands* don't mean "then to" or "next," as though Jesus was advocating a strategy of sequential steps. All the regions were to have the apostles' attention and efforts simultaneously. This same strategy is important in today's globalized age, with its exponential international migration, in which people from every tribe, tongue, and nation are crisscrossing the world right to our doorstep. Our witness needs to be right *here* where we are, it needs to be *nearby*, and it needs to be *over there* at the same time.

A Missiological Parsing of Acts 1:8

This verse also provides a glimpse into the dynamics involved when the gospel travels from place to place and culture to culture. The paradigm of the disciples starting out from the city of Jerusalem is portrayed in the following chart. Notice the dynamics, which all cross-cultural workers need to pay close attention to in regard to ethnicity, geography, language, and culture.

Dynamic	In Jerusalem and in all Judea	and Samaria	and to the end of the earth
Ethnicity	Their own people	Mixed race of Jews and Gentiles	Other peoples altogether
Geography	Their own capital city and regional identity	Neighboring region	Far-away places
Language	Their native language (difference in accent only)	Different dialect	Completely foreign language
Culture	Their own culture	Slightly different culture	Significantly different cultures

The genius of Christianity is that God can genuinely be worshipped wherever believers are found, in ways that are culturally appropriate to them.

Three Types of Evangelism

Ralph Winter, in his historic address at the 1974 Lausanne International Congress on World Evangelization, did his generation of believers a great service by helping them understand the missiological paradigm Jesus gave in Acts 1:8. In that address, Winter pinpointed three types of evangelism needed to reach the world, labeling them E-1, E-2, and E-3 evangelism.[61]

E-1 evangelism takes place when a person stays within his own people group, geographic area, language, and culture to win people to Christ. This happens, for example, when a Caucasian American witnesses to another Caucasian American living down the street. With most everything in common between them, the task of communicating is relatively easy and without barriers.

In E-2 evangelism, the task is not as simple and requires different techniques. The bearer of the gospel crosses into a different, but usually nearby, geographical area to reach people who speak a different, yet understandable, dialect and who are living within a slightly different culture. The cultural and linguistic barriers crossed are relatively simple to navigate. A Navajo believer going to the Apache would be an example.

E-3 evangelism requires a more complicated communication skill set because of the higher barriers that need to be crossed. In this instance, a Christ-follower goes to an altogether different people, who usually live in a distant place, speak a completely different language, and operate in a completely foreign culture. The messenger must engage in language acquisition, cultural adaptation, and worldview comprehension before she is able to present the gospel with clarity and effectiveness. The task is considerably more difficult than E-1 or E-2 evangelism and typically demands special training. A Canadian going to the Lisu people of southern China would be an example.

Although there are differences in the complexity of the task, E-1, E-2, and E-3 are to be seen as equal in value, but not necessarily in priority, as we endeavor to reach A Third of Us. We can only reach the remaining 3.2 billion by engaging in E-3 outreach.

---

61 *Perspectives on the World Christian Movement*, edited by Ralph D. Winter and Steven C. Hawthorne, 339–53.

With this explanation, another look at the parsing of Acts 1:8 reveals the following:

Dynamic	In Jerusalem and in all Judea	and Samaria	and to the end of the earth
Ethnicity	Their own people	Mixed race of Jews and Gentiles	Other peoples altogether
Geography	Their own capital city and regional identity	Neighboring region	Far-away places
Language	Their native language (difference in accent only)	Different dialect	Completely foreign language
Culture	Their own culture	Slightly different culture	Significantly different cultures
Type of Evangelism	E-1 Evangelism	E-2 Evangelism	E-3 Evangelism

E-1 evangelism is powerful, but E-2 and E-3 evangelism are essential to reaching the unreached. Fully one-third of the world's 7.8 billion people—A Third of Us—cannot be reached unless the church engages in E-3 evangelism. Another third, which are "close by," cannot be reached without E-2 evangelism. Winter aptly said, "We are forced to believe that until every tribe and tongue has a strong, powerfully evangelizing church in it, and thus E-1 witness within it, E-2 and E-3 efforts coming from outside are still essential and highly urgent."[62]

The Means of Human Instrumentality

One last comment needs to be made about the disciples' (and our!) personal involvement. Jesus put at the heart of the commission this phrase:

" *... and you will be my witnesses ... "*

Human instrumentality is the God-ordained means of reaching out to humans. No other way, avenue, or being was enlisted by God to do this task. It takes humans reaching humans for this mission to be most successful. That is why, to quote from *The Manifesto for the Unreached*, we affirm: "We refuse to stand idly by as people enter eternity without Christ when we can share the good news that transforms them through any means possible." (See the appendix.)

---

62 Winter, *Perspectives*, 345. For a fuller discussion of the implications of the three kinds of evangelism, read Dr. Winter's entire address in *Perspectives*. Winter brings up the issue of "people blindness," which relates directly to the unfinished task.

It takes humans reaching humans for this mission to be most successful.

British missionary William Carey, the "father of modern missions," had to persuade a denomination of reluctant Baptists to get involved in world evangelization. To convince them of its importance, he wrote a pamphlet that used the word *means* in its title. In it, after discussing the importance of the "means of prayer," he wrote:

We must not be contented however with praying, without exerting ourselves in the use of means for the obtaining of those things we pray for. Were the children of light but as wise in their generation as the children of this world they would stretch every nerve to gain so glorious a prize, nor ever imagine that it was to be obtained in any other way. [63]

The disciples had been eyewitnesses of Jesus' life and ministry from the very start. These men had spent three full years with him, which allowed them to observe him under every conceivable circumstance. They witnessed every miracle he performed and heard every address he spoke. They saw his concern for the lost, his compassion for the unfortunate, and his care of the needy. They listened to his beautifully crafted parables and saw him dumbfound his critics with his wisdom. And in the end, they watched as he suffered and died, but also met with him several times after he victoriously rose from the dead. For them, the claim that Jesus was the Son of God was indisputable. [64]

Thus the disciples needed no persuasion that Jesus' words and works were of God. They had witnessed every aspect of his life and ministry. They were eyewitnesses when all those marvelous things transpired. Indeed, Jesus was that "which we have heard, which we have seen with our eyes, which we looked upon and have touched with our hands" (1 John 1:1). As eyewitnesses, they could testify to the veracity of all Jesus' mighty acts.

When Jesus told them that they would now "be my witnesses," he was telling them that they were to proclaim what they had personally experienced with him. Their story was linked to their identification with him. Their firsthand experiences would lend credence to their message.

---

63 In 1792, Carey wrote these words in his eighty-seven-page pamphlet, *An Enquiry into the Obligation of Christians to Use Means for the Conversion of the Heathens*. His arguments were convincing enough that the Particular Baptists agreed to set up a sending agency, Baptist Missionary Society (the first of its kind in the English-speaking world), and send Carey and his wife, Dorothy, as their first missionaries to India the following year.

64 J. Herbert Kane, *Christian Missions in Biblical Perspective*, 54.

Over the centuries, the meaning of the word *witness* (*martures*) has evolved in Christian circles. It has moved from its original, generic meaning of "somebody who saw or heard something happen and gives evidence about it" to the more specific meaning of "a public statement of strong personal Christian beliefs." Because so many believers have died doing that very thing, the word eventually took on the meaning of "martyr." A martyr is a believer who has lost his or her life prematurely in a situation of witness, as a result of human hostility. According to Christian tradition, every one of the apostles, with the exception of John, would die a martyr's death.

This is the kind of witness Jesus would have us making as we go to the unreached. Christ's mission to the nations can only go forward as believers proclaim what they themselves have personally experienced with Christ. It is those believers who boldly give public affirmation about their salvation experience and believe in it so strongly that they are even prepared to die a martyr's death who push outreach forward. This is what Jesus' disciples ended up spending the rest of their lives doing. This is what believers in every age should be willing to do as well.

REACHING A THIRD OF US

The daunting task of world evangelization that lay before the disciples would take more muscle than they could ever muster in and of themselves. As well trained as they were, after spending three years with Jesus, they lacked the one important ingredient that would enable them to be message-bearers with confidence. They needed the supernatural empowerment from a higher source, the Holy Spirit. He alone would enable them to carry on the task. Jesus was now ready to send the Holy Spirit to them, as he left them permanently.

Just before his final departure, Jesus told his disciples about the strategic means in which the gospel was to go forth from Jerusalem. First, they were to proclaim it within their own general environs. Then they were to take it across ethnic barriers to nearby peoples. Finally, they were to cross over into foreign cultures and peoples who were vastly different than themselves. But as they went farther and farther, they were not to forget the previously evangelized areas. Simultaneously, these areas were to have their attention as well.

The gospel message is applicable to all peoples everywhere at all times. It is a supra-cultural message that finds meaningful acceptance wherever it is proclaimed. Therefore, the disciples' task was not complete until they had carried it to the uttermost parts of the earth. And if they failed to complete that task in their lifetime, then those who followed after them were to pick up where they left off. That would be us.

CHAPTER 8

Why Reach a Third of Us?

"For God so loved the world,
that he gave his only Son,
that whoever believes in him should not perish
but have eternal life."   —John 3:16

everal years ago I was flying out of central China to Beijing to catch a connecting flight back to the States. Seated in the seats next to me were two elderly professors, husband and wife, who were on the faculty of Beijing University. They were friendly, and I could tell they were eager to use their English, which, by the way, was pretty good. I had just completed a series of meetings with Christian leaders in a city of Shanxi province. Sitting there, they must have been wondering what would bring a foreigner like me to such a remote part of their country.

We engaged in typical chitchat for a while until curiosity got the better of them. They finally asked me outright why I had traveled so far from home to speak to their people and about what. I knew that as professors at a prestigious government university they could only have their positions by being members of the Communist Party. So, I told them outright that I had been speaking to a group of Christians to encourage them in their faith. Intrigued, they then asked what would motivate me to do such a thing.

I thought about that for a moment and then responded slowly and deliberately with "Because ... God so loved the world, that he gave his only Son, that whoever believes in him should not perish but have eternal life." Upon hearing those words, they said that they had heard them once before, during their younger years as university students in Japan. But they didn't understand their meaning.

The Popularity of John 3:16

John 3:16 is considered the most popular and arguably the most recited verse of the entire Bible. It is without question the most translated piece of literature in the world. It is usually the verse first memorized by new believers or by children in Sunday school. I have seen it hanging on the walls of church nurseries and even in the palace of a king.[65] I have seen it transcribed into dozens of tribal dialects, hanging individually on plaques on the wall of a mission office on the island of Papua, Indonesia, signifying that a Bible translation project was currently underway in that language.

Most likely you have seen it displayed in public too. You have may have seen it on giant banners at football stadiums or etched into eye smear

---

65 This is literally true. When visiting in northern Cameroon with a group of graduate students, we were invited into the palace of "the Fonz," the king of Okuland. He was a Christian king, and a former pastor. There on the center of the wall behind his throne in bold letters was John 3:16 fully written out.

of football players on national television.[66] Perhaps on the freeway, either pasted on giant billboards or whizzing by you on a car's "vanity plate." Yes, John 3:16 is the most recognizable verse of all of Scripture.

Why is this verse so venerated among believers? Because it encapsulates the heart of the gospel like no other. The reason for reaching the unreached is because of the clear-cut message of John 3:16. This one verse is a lucid summary of the entire gospel.[67] If the whole Bible were to be summed up in one verse, this would be it.[68]

The message of John 3:16 is the reason for reaching A Third of Us. If it did not exist, neither would the need for outreach. There would be no need to go anywhere. There would be no need to make disciples.

Although all believers have a sentimental belief in John 3:16, many seem not to have a substantive belief in it.

There would be no need to baptize, teach, or plant churches. There would be no need to make sacrifices for Jesus, because Jesus would not have sacrificed his life for us. But we know the opposite to be true. The truth of John 3:16 is a reality that happened. It is the reason for seeking the lost.

However, I have discovered from my experiences of speaking in churches across North America that although all believers have a sentimental belief in John 3:16, many seem not to have a substantive belief in it. In other words, many believers can recite the verse from memory and have good feelings about it, but when quizzed about the precise meaning of what it teaches, they become confused or uncertain.

Unknown to most, the greatest theological uncertainty in the minds of members of the North American church today is the meaning of this verse. It seems that, secretly, most would like to believe otherwise. Rather than affirming the exclusive message of the cross for man's salvation, many would prefer to believe that somehow, in some way, some people, somewhere, by

---

66 University of Florida quarterback Tim Tebow, a missionary kid, devout believer, and arguably the best college quarterback ever in the history of the game, etched "John" under one eye and 3:16 under the other in the 2008 FedEx BCS National Championship game. It wasn't hard for television cameras to pick it up, and believers around the country were thrilled to see this bold testimony.

67 Timothy George, "Big-Picture Faith," *Christianity Today*, October 23, 2000.

68 This can be said categorically because of the theology contained therein. Of the nine divisions of systematic theology, five are mentioned: 1) Theology proper: "God," as the source of salvation; 2) Anthropology: "world" (since man is the apex of the created order), the object of salvation; 3) Christology: "his Son," the means of salvation; 4) Soteriology: "whoever believes," the appropriation of salvation; and 5) Eschatology: "should not perish but have eternal life," the benefit of salvation.

To hold such a belief— that of equating the God of Scripture with other gods—is to misunderstand and misrepresent God as he has revealed himself to us.

some other means, can be saved and make it to heaven following an alternate route outside of personal belief in the redemptive work of Christ for sin.

How is this manifested? By asking some probing questions about the verse that many find difficult to answer. Five questions that come straight out of the verse will help clarify what it means. These questions are based on the words of the text itself. Red-letter edition Bibles typically mark this verse in red, signifying that Jesus spoke these words. However, this probably was not the case. Many commentators believe that Jesus' words ended with verse 15 and verses 16 and following is a reflection from John himself.[69]

Here is the question for us: What would Jesus have us know about the gospel from this one sentence? A look at the words themselves helps us discover God's intent by way of the following questions.

Five Probing Questions Related to John 3:16

1. "For God ..."

Is the God of the Bible the same god of other religions, just shrouded in different names and attributes by humans, but in essence the same god?

This is a good place to start, because so many are confused on this point. Some claim that the God who has revealed himself in the Christian Scriptures is the identical god of most every religion. It is just that Christians call him God, whereas others call him by some other name. The Muslims call him Allah, the Hindus call him Brahman, the Buddhists call him Buddha (at least some branches do), and neo-pagans call her Mother Earth, Pan, Artemis, Isis, etc. So it really doesn't matter what god you pray to, because in reality every deity is ultimately the same deity, just shrouded in different names and attributes by mankind. Consequently, it is common to hear even believers say, "We Christians pray to the same God as Muslims."

---

69 NIV Application Commentary: "Many scholars agree that 3:16–21 provides reflections or meditations written by John. This means that ... the quotation marks should end at 3:15, where Jesus uses his characteristic title "Son of Man." Note that in 3:16 Jesus' death is described as past (God gave his one and only Son), and much of the language of these verses is distinctly Johannine. With verse 16 we are reading John's commentary on the importance of Jesus' words to Nicodemus."

To hold such a belief—that of equating the God of Scripture with other gods—is to misunderstand and misrepresent God as he has revealed himself to us. It disguises who God really is and, furthermore, taints his image.

It would be like being invited to the White House for a masquerade party, where everyone is asked to dress in costumes and masks to look like the president. Imagine hundreds of presidential look-alikes! Although some attendees would come very close to replicating the president and maybe even fool some into believing he/she was the president, there still would be only one authentic president present, whom everyone else copied. When it was time for the masks to come off and the costumes discarded, only one genuine person, the president himself, would be left standing as the real, indisputable president of the United States. Pretenders would be revealed for what they really were—just imitations.

So it is with God. Although there are many pretenders, and some that are remarkably convincing counterfeits, in reality there is only one God who alone stands as the true God. This one true God is the God who has revealed himself in Scripture as the Triune God, Creator of the universe, distinct from creation but in control of it.

There are several ways that God sets himself apart from all other gods.

By his revelation

All other religions are out to discover who god is, whereas the God of Scripture has disclosed who he is to mankind. Only in the Judeo-Christian Scriptures do we find a God of revelation who goes to great lengths to disclose himself. Our responsibility is to read and believe God's revelation about himself to gain an understanding of who he is. Nothing additional can be known about God other than what he has revealed about himself in his written Word. It is left to his followers, then, to read, believe, and personally apply his disclosure about himself to get to know God better.

Adherents of other religions have a much more difficult task. They must "discover" their god though subjective means. Some of those religions have the benefit of their scripture to help; but these, by their own admission, are incomplete and in need of additional discovery beyond them to better understand transcendence. Therefore, their quest leads them to seek transcendence through personal enlightenment, mystical communion, transcendental meditation, or the arbitrary word of a religious practitioner (such as a mullah or a medium) to help discover their god. That is why there is such a variety of concepts of deity even within the same religion.

By his claim of exclusiveness

God is not to be compared to any other god. He is not one god among the gods, or the best god among all the gods. He alone is God. It grieves him to be compared to a being who is less than himself. In the Old Testament, Israel's persistent idolatry caused God to categorically declare these truths about himself:

> I am the LORD; that is my name; my glory I give to no other, nor my praise to carved idols. Isaiah 42:8

> Before me no god was formed, none shall there be any after me.
> I, I am the LORD, and besides me there is no savior. Isaiah 43:10–11

> I am the first and I am the last; besides me there is no god. Isaiah 44:6

> Is there a God besides me? There is no Rock; I know not any. Isaiah 44:8

> I am the LORD, and there is no other, besides me there is no God; I equip you, though you do not know me, that people may know, from the rising of the sun and from the west, that there is none besides me; I am the LORD, and there is no other. Isaiah 45:5–6.

By his commandment

God commanded that there be no rival to him since he alone is the one true God. To believe otherwise is to violate the first command of the Ten Commandments: "You shall have no other gods before me" (Ex 20:3). Although people, being religious by nature, have a concept of the divine, that concept is corrupted if it is not in agreement with what God has revealed about himself in Scripture. He commands that no other god ever be equated with him.

Just because people use religion to equate God with other gods, that is not a valid excuse for degrading God into the image man conceives him to be. German theologian Erich Saurer insightfully noted this connection with the first commandment. Writing in an era that used terminology (i.e., *heathen*) we shy away from today, he said this:

> In his religion the heathen expresses his godlessness. Religion itself is the sin, namely the sin against the first command, the replacing of God by the gods, the most powerful expression of the opposition of man against God and contradiction within himself."

So is the God who reveals himself in Scripture the same god who is worshipped in other religions? No, he is not! "But," one may ask, "if another religion is monotheistic like Christianity, couldn't their god be the same as ours?" No, absolutely not. The reason this cannot be is because other monotheistic religions describe God in terms and concepts that contradict what the true and living God has revealed about himself. The god(s) of other religions is too limited (Islam), too many (Hinduism), too human-like (New Age), too transcendent (animism), or too much a figment of man's imagination (Buddhism)!

2. "... so loved the world ..."
If God is a God of love, doesn't he save people based on that love?
Those who raise this question hold a very common misconception of this attribute of God. Behind the question is the belief that God is so full of love that everything he does must be governed by that love. The problem with this view of God is that it makes him out to be a benevolent grandfather-type of Being who makes light of his high standards, which in turn contradicts his holy nature. While it is true that God by his very nature is love, that love is not an excuse for him to permit evil and sin to go unchecked in his holy presence.

If one attribute is singled out as God's overriding attribute, it would have to be his holiness. All of his other attributes, as expressed toward man (love, justice, compassion, etc.), fall in line with and never contradict his holiness. It is sin that separates man from God and his holy presence, something that even a loving God cannot overlook. Scripture presents the issue this way:

1) **No person is innocent in their sin.** "Therefore, just as sin came into the world through one man, and death through sin, and so death spread to all men because all sinned" (Rom 5:12).
2) **God hates sin and those who commit it.** "The boastful shall not stand before your eyes; you hate all evildoers" (Ps 5:5).
3) **Every person, as a sinful human being, is alienated from God because of that sin.** "And you, who once were alienated and hostile in mind, doing evil deeds, he has now reconciled in his body of flesh by his death, in order to present you holy and blameless and above reproach before him" (Col 1:21–22).
4) **Our common sinful humanity, regardless of our religious upbringing, separates us from God.** Therefore, God has provided love on his terms.

His great love provided a way for man to circumvent the curse of his sin and establish a relationship with him. The apostle John states it clearly: "... God is love. In this the love of God was made manifest among us, that God sent his only Son into the world, so that we might live through him. In this is love, not that we have loved God but that he loved us and sent his Son to be the propitiation for our sins" (1 John 4:8–10).

5) **By his very nature, God is love; but he demonstrates his love toward mankind on his terms:** "God shows his love for us in that while we were still sinners, Christ died for us" (Rom 5:8).

God's love permitted propitiation to be made for man's sins. His love combined with his holiness demanded a sacrifice—not a wishy-washy, automatically accept "whatever" and give a blanket pardon kind of love. God's holiness had to be satisfied, and out of love he satisfied it through the sacrifice of his Son. So, no, God does not save people based on his love. He saves people based on his loving provision.

3. "... that he gave his only Son ..."
If Jesus died for the world, then isn't everyone already saved based on his death for all mankind?

This line of reasoning is rooted in a type of universalism that is sometimes call neo-universalism. Though it takes the Bible seriously and is Trinitarian, it teaches that all will ultimately be saved based on Christ's provision. Its proponents believe that Jesus was indeed God and that he died for all people and purposes for all people to be saved. Therefore, all will be saved by the merit of Christ's death, for Christ died for all.

The difficulty with this view is that it ignores the conditional clause that follows it: "that whoever believes in him ..." Every human being is responsible to make a conscious response to Christ's redeeming work. That response is belief—belief that Jesus' sacrifice was enough to satisfy God's wrath for one's personal sin.

It is true that salvation is made available to all, but it is not true that it is automatically applicable (efficacious) to all. The work of Christ demands a faith response by each individual as an acknowledgement of acceptance and allegiance to Christ. Notice how many times the faith

God does not save people based on his love. He saves people based on his loving provision.

response of "believe" is mentioned in the following verse: "Whoever believes in him is not condemned, but whoever does not believe is condemned already, because he has not believed in the name of the only Son of God" (John 3:18). The human response of belief is requisite for salvation.

John 3:16 is a beautiful summary of the entire gospel in fewer than thirty words. If the whole Bible had been destroyed or lost, except for John 3:16, that would still be enough for any person to come to know God and to receive eternal life.
—Timothy George

To put it another way, God's salvation is available to all, but accepted only by some. In theological terms, there is unlimited atonement but limited application. No, everyone is not automatically saved based on Christ's redemptive work. There is a message to be believed and a conscious response to be made.

4. "... that whoever believes in him ..."
Aren't there other ways leading to God besides believing in Jesus?
To discredit the uniqueness of Jesus has been the quest of every major religion since the days he walked this earth. Judaism and Islam seem to be the most intent on doing this, but neo-paganism and others, like New Age spiritualists, are not far behind. The goal of discrediting Jesus' uniqueness is also to discredit his unique redemptive work. "Certainly," some suggest, "there must be alternative ways leading to God other than through the exclusive redemptive work of Jesus Christ. How can there possibly be only one way?"

"After all," they contend, "doesn't that position smack of elitism, privilege, and even spiritual bigotry? Wouldn't the Hindu scriptures be more palatable that say, 'Howsoever man may approach me, even so do I accept them; for on all sides, whatever path they may choose is mine?'" (Bhagavad-Gita, iv.11).

Many people today prefer to customize their religious beliefs, drawing from a smorgasbord of religious options. For them, it isn't a matter of choosing one path, but the mixing of paths. To eclectically choose from an assortment of beliefs in order to personalize one's own beliefs is in vogue as a sign of intelligent "spirituality."

The apostle Peter said something much different. Standing before a group of distinguished religious scholars, he said,

There is salvation in no one else, for there is no other name under heaven given among men by which we must be saved. —Acts 4:12

Previously, Peter had heard Jesus proclaim, "I am the way, and the truth, and the life. No one comes to the Father except through me" (John 14:6). Peter now elaborates on that declaration by saying two things that are helpful to those who have an inkling that somehow, somewhere, some people can come by some other means to God.

First, he says that geographically, no matter where one may go on this earth—whether it be deep into the jungles of the Amazon basin or to the top of the Himalayas—there is no people located anywhere "under heaven" that have discovered another name whereby they can be saved. The persistent, romantic belief that somewhere in the distant reaches of the earth other cultures may have found a way to gain acceptance by God through a means other than Jesus Christ is not plausible.

No, there are no other ways leading to God besides through Jesus Christ. He alone can save.

Looking at the issue another way, the second thing Peter says is that there is no group of people or ethnic group of humanity ("given among men") that has discovered salvation apart from Christ. Whether they be the Minangkabau of Sumatra, mentioned in chapter 1, or the Macedonians of Europe, no people group has discovered a way to have a right relationship with God within themselves. Anthropologists tell us that there are just over seventeen thousand ethno-linguistic people groups in the world. Peter says that not one of them, even though they be many (so the chances are great), has discovered salvation outside of belief in Christ.

These two phrases—"that he gave his only Son" and "that whoever believes in him"—press the claim of the universal need for Jesus to the fullest extent.[70] Salvation is found in Christ alone. All peoples, no matter where they reside or what belief system they hold, must "believe in him." So, to answer the question at hand: No, there are no other ways leading to God besides through Jesus Christ. He alone can save.

---

70 John Piper, *Let the Nations Be Glad!* (Grand Rapids: Baker Academic, 2003), 141.

5. "... should not perish but have eternal life."
Aren't nonbelievers annihilated, or simply extinguished, at death?

John 3:16 certainly makes it look like at the time of death, some people (nonbelievers) are annihilated, whereas other people (believers) keep living forever. But that is not what the end of the verse is saying. The Greek word *apolumi*, translated here as "perish," can just as readily be translated "separated" or "set apart." Those who die without believing in Jesus will perish in the sense that they will be separated from God. Their destiny is not obliteration, but rather a continued existence of ruin outside of God's presence forever.

The thought of such a destiny is both sobering and heart-wrenching. Believers should never take pleasure in the condemnation of the lost, no matter how bad the person might have been in this life. Divine retribution is a terrible thing—something that all deserve, but all want to avoid. And here is why: Just as eternal life is everlasting, so eternal separation is everlasting too.

For some theologians, the thought of nonbelievers experiencing eternal conscious punishment is intolerable.[71] They believe John 3:16 teaches that although the reward for belief is eternal life, the punishment for unbelief is eternal annihilation. For them, God does not raise the wicked from the dead in order to consciously torture them forever, but rather to declare his judgment upon them and then condemn them to extinction, which is "the second death."[72]

However, there are many passages in Scripture that say otherwise. Of all people, Jesus had more to say about hell as a place of eternal conscious punishment than anyone else (Matt 3:12; 18:8; 25:41, 46; Mark 9:43–48). To help drive home his point, he told a sobering parable about the rich man and Lazarus (Luke 16:19–31). From that parable, six truths about death are evident:

---

71 John Stott, in his honesty, struggled with this concept. "Emotionally, I find the concept (of eternal conscious punishment) intolerable and do not understand how people can live with it without either cauterizing their feelings or cracking under the strain. David Edwards, with a response from John Stott, *Evangelical Essentials: A Liberal-Evangelical Dialogue* (Downers Grove, IL: InterVarsity Press, 1988), 314–20.

72 This is the view of Clark Pinnock in "Fire, Then Nothing," *Christianity Today* 44, no. 10 (March 20, 1987): 49.

1) There is continued existence after physical death.

2) There is a separate destiny for believers and nonbelievers.

3) That destiny is final.

4) The decision is made in this life as to where one spends eternity.

5) People cannot transfer from one place of destiny to another—the location is irrevocably set at the time of death.

6) Once in hell a person cannot send a messenger to warn loved ones; it is too late for that to be done. Living loved ones must be informed and warned by the living.

Wrapping It Up

The following statement summarizes what John 3:16 and other Scriptures teach in regard to salvation: Salvation is found in no one else, but is based solely on the merits of the historic, finished work of the sinless Christ on the cross on behalf of sinful mankind. We must consciously place our faith (trust) in Christ's redemptive work, and thus experience a personal conversion, in order to be saved.

This statement takes the following set of beliefs into account:

1) All humans are sinners, by nature and by choice, and are therefore guilty and under divine condemnation.

2) Salvation is only through Christ and his atoning work.

3) Belief is necessary to obtain the salvation achieved by Christ. Therefore, believers have a responsibility to tell unbelievers the good news about Jesus Christ.

4) Adherents of other religions, no matter how sincere their belief or how zealous their religious activity, are spiritually lost apart from Christ.

5) Physical death brings to an end the opportunity to exercise saving faith and acceptance of Jesus. The decisions made in this life are irrevocably fixed at death.

6) At the great final judgment, all humans will be separated on the basis of their relationship to Christ during this life. Those who have believed in him will spend eternity in everlasting joy and

reward in God's presence. Those who have not accepted him will experience a place of unending suffering, where they will be eternally separated from God.

The following story about a mousetrap helps to tie the importance of John 3:16 to the need to evangelize the unreached.

The Mouse Trap
(Author Unknown)

A mouse looked through the crack in the wall to see the farmer and his wife open a package.

What food might this contain? the mouse wondered. He was devastated to discover it was a mousetrap. Retreating to the farmyard, the mouse proclaimed the warning. "There is a mousetrap in the house! There is a mousetrap in the house!"

The chicken clucked and scratched, raised her head and said, "Mr. Mouse, I can tell this is a grave concern to you, but it is of no consequence to me. I cannot be bothered by it."

The mouse turned to the pig and told him, "There is a mousetrap in the house! There is a mousetrap in the house!" The pig sympathized, but said, "I am so very sorry, Mr. Mouse, but there is nothing I can do about it but pray. Be assured you are in my prayers."

The mouse turned to the cow and said, "There is a mousetrap in the house! There is a mousetrap in the house!" The cow said, "Wow, Mr. Mouse. I'm sorry for you, but it's no skin off my nose."

So, the mouse returned to the house, head down and dejected, to face the farmer's mousetrap alone.

That very night a sound was heard throughout the house—like the sound of a mousetrap catching its prey. The farmer's wife rushed to see what was caught. In the darkness, she did not see it was a venomous snake whose tail the trap had caught. The snake bit the farmer's wife. The farmer rushed her back to bed, but she began to get hot with fever.

Everyone knows you treat a fever with fresh chicken soup, so the farmer took his hatchet to the farmyard for the soup's main ingredient. But his wife's sickness continued, so friends and neighbors came to sit with her around the clock. To feed them, the farmer went out to the barnyard and butchered the pig.

The farmer's wife did not get well; she died. So many people came for her funeral; the farmer had the cow slaughtered to provide enough meat for all. The mouse looked upon it all from his crack in the wall with great sadness and just shook his head in bewilderment.

What's the moral as it relates to this discussion? Simply this: John 3:16 is at the core of all of Christian theology. We must beware, unless—like the "harmless" mousetrap—it is ignored, denied, or considered of little consequence. It is at the center of God's redemptive plan. To deny it is to threaten all of Christian theology. Therefore, with *The Manifesto for the Unreached*, we strongly affirm: "We will shout from every peak, pinnacle and rooftop that the only hope for this dying world is a relationship with Jesus Christ." (See the appendix.)

REACHING A THIRD OF US

John 3:16 is both the logical and theological reason for reaching the unreached. This verse tells us why we do it. It explains the source of salvation (God); his motive for granting salvation (love); the object of his salvation (the world); his provision of salvation (his only Son); the way to appropriate salvation (believe in him); and the benefit of salvation (not perish but have eternal life). The entire gospel is encapsulated in this one verse.

CHAPTER 9

Opposition to Reaching a Third of Us

"There is no neutral ground in the universe. Every square inch, every split second, is claimed by God and counterclaimed by Satan." —C. S. Lewis

"I know enough about Satan to realize that he will have all his weapons ready for determined opposition. He would be a missionary simpleton who expected plain sailing in any work of God." —James O. Fraser

Those who engage in reaching the final unreached peoples will experience opposition and hostility.[73] After all, one of the main reasons they are still unreached is because they are located in areas of the world that are the most hostile to the Christian message. Message-bearers must consider the cost to their well-being as they contemplate their part in taking the gospel to the remaining A Third of Us.

It can be costly to serve as one of Jesus' messengers. For some it can be very costly. The gospel of Jesus is so countercultural that it stands as a threat to the prevailing worldview of every culture it encounters. In return, gatekeepers of those cultures threaten back as the gospel makes inroads into their area of influence. They instigate backlashes and resistance that are manifested in acts of opposition, persecution, and at times even in the taking of lives.

> **It can be costly to serve as one of Jesus' messengers. For some it can be very costly.**

Counting the Cost

Andrew Walls reminds us that Jesus took for granted that there would be rubs and friction accompanying our witness—not from the adoption of a different culture that the gospel can bring, but from the transformation of the mind of those who believe in Christ. Accordingly, the follower of Jesus inherits

> the pilgrim principle, which whispers to him that he has no abiding city and warns him that to be faithful to Christ will put him out of step with his society; for that society never existed, in East or West, ancient time or modern, which could absorb the word of Christ painlessly into its system.[74]

If that be the case in general, how much more for messenger-bearers who are willing to go cross-culturally.

With this perspective in mind, when it came to sending his disciples out into this fallen and hostile world, Jesus made three things perfectly clear: 1) he would not send them out with carelessness; 2) he would not send them out comfortless and; 3) he would not send them out clueless about the types and depths of opposition they would encounter.

73 This chapter first appeared in *Sorrow and Blood: Christian Mission in Contexts of Suffering, Persecution, and Martyrdom*, edited by William D. Taylor, Antonia ver der Meer, and Reg Reimer (Pasadena, CA: William Carey Library, 2012).

74 Andrew Walls, *The Missionary Movement in Christian History* (Maryknoll, New York: Orbis Books, 2005), 8.

Opposition and persecution was a reality about which Jesus had a lot to say, because he knew his messengers would experience it a lot. Divinely discerning the times, he knew that in every age his ambassadors would encounter opposition as they engaged the world on his behalf. His mission would be conducted in the context of confrontation. Engaging the hearts of humankind would demand engaging an even greater power in the sphere of spiritual warfare. There are always casualties in warfare. It is always costly for those who participate in it.

The discourse of Jesus found in Matthew 10 is a benchmark for understanding opposition, persecution, and martyrdom in the context of world evangelization. By it, Jesus candidly covers the topic rather exhaustively. Why did he so painstakingly focus on this topic? Because he wanted to make sure that the disciples who first heard it, and all his messengers who would follow after them, would know what they would face as they went forth. Consequently, this pointed instruction serves as a template on opposition for gospel-bearing messengers of all ages.

In Matthew 10 we see Jesus for the first time sending his disciples out on a mission—albeit a short-term assignment. This would serve as a "trial-run" or "warm-up" mission for the greater worldwide mission they would initiate after Jesus' ascension into heaven. Notice all that he says about the resistance they would encounter.

Realities of Persecution

First, Jesus informs his followers that not all persecution is equally intense or carries equal consequences. Believers experience various degrees of resistance, with martyrdom as the ultimate possibility.

Degrees of Persecution

As Jesus was sending out his disciples, he explicitly cautioned that they could face up to six degrees of opposition.

Jesus used six phrases to describe the increasingly intense hostilities that opposition can take. He begins with the least severe form of hostility and then progresses in ascending order to the ultimate experience. Christ shows that his messengers could expect to be: prevented outright from proclaiming the gospel ("will not welcome you,"[75] v. 14); rejected if given opportunity ("or listen to your words," v. 14); detained ("hand you over," v. 17; "arrest

---

75 All the Scripture references in this chapter are from the New International Version, 1984 edition.

you," v. 19); physically abused ("flog you," v. 17); pursued with intent to harm ("you are persecuted," v. 23); and finally, martyred ("kill the body," v. 28). When viewed graphically, the incremental progression becomes clear.

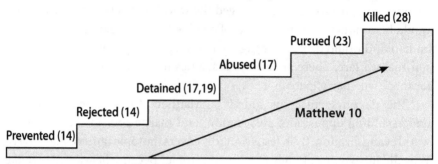

Notice that losing one's life as a result of human hostility in a situation of witness is the ultimate hostile experience. Lest one be tempted to shy away from service because of the possibility of experiencing this ultimate trial—martyrdom—a word on this most severe form of opposition is needful.

You may recall the story of pioneer missionary John Allen Chau, who at age twenty-seven died at the hands of the Sentinelese peoples of the Andaman archipelago (India) in November 2018. The Sentinelese tribe that John had a passion to reach remains one of the most isolated, unengaged, and unreached people groups in the world. When he arrived on their beach, they brutally killed him with spear and arrow. John had prepared himself for years to reach them, and even admitted that he felt contacting them might bring about his death. But he went anyway. As with the five Auca martyrs in the jungles of Ecuador in 1956, John's martyrdom acted as a catalyst for some to dedicate their lives to reaching unreached peoples.

Martyrdom is not something a person usually anticipates nor to which one readily aspires. It is an experience that God, in his providence, bestows on select individuals for purposes ultimately known only to him. Yet the premature death of a follower of Christ as a result of human hostility has an enduring impact on observant believers. It causes most to pause and ponder anew the extreme cost of discipleship. It forces many to question whether they themselves measure up to the highest standard of devotion to Christ and his cause. It motivates still others to abandon selfish plans and ambitions and turn to serve Christ in hard and difficult places. It creates a baseline for the church from which to measure its worth—i.e., whether its activities are meaningful and truly important in light of death and eternity. We need to be cognizant of the fact that martyrdom has multiple values.

Sources of Persecution

Jesus did not want his messengers to be either surprised or naïve about the sources from which opposition would come. He delineates four specific sources that messengers need to beware of and consider with guarded prudence. He cautioned that opposition would spring from *the community* ("Be on your guard against men; they will hand you over ..." v. 17); *the state* ("you will be brought before governors and kings," v. 18); *religious leaders* ("hand you over to the local councils and flog you in their synagogues," v. 17); and even from those most dear to them—members of their own *family* ("Brother will betray brother to death, and a father his child ...," v. 21).

In his foreknowledge of the global context of world evangelism, Jesus informs us that in reality there is no safe haven or refuge within a society and no level of authority within a community that should not be considered a potential oppressor.

Attitude behind Persecution

What is the underlying attitude that drives nonbelievers to oppose and oppress God's messengers? Jesus sums it up in one word: *hate* ("All men will *hate* you because of me," v. 22). The form of the verb Jesus used here shows this hatred to be ongoing, and can better read: "You will continually be hated because of me." Unqualified hatred has been the hardened heart's emotional response to Jesus through the ages. Why is this? Because his message is a threat to preferred lifestyles and orientations. Mankind hates the light (John 3:20) and the source of light (John 15:20); thus their ongoing disdain for bearers of the light.

Later, in a more sober setting, Jesus painted a fuller picture of this Satan-generated hatred. Fast-forward to the evening of his crucifixion. Jesus proclaimed that the world's hatred of his emissaries was intricately tied to its hatred of him. In John 15:18–25, Jesus declared:

> *If the world hates you, keep in mind that it hated me first. If you belonged to the world, it would love you as its own. As it is, you do not belong to the world, but I have chosen you out of the world. That is why the world hates you. Remember the words I spoke to you: "No servant is greater than his master." If they persecuted me, they will persecute you also... . They will treat you*

this way because of my name, for they do not know the One who sent me.... He who hates me hates my Father as well. If I had not done among them what no one else did, they would not be guilty of sin. But now they have seen these miracles, and yet they have hated both me and my Father. But this is to fulfill what is written in their Law: "They hated me without reason."

Response of the Messenger to Persecution

With these three realities clarified, how should Christ's messengers conduct themselves as they go forth heralding his message? Again, in Matthew 10, Jesus mentions three appropriate responses.

Prudence

> The destruction of one's own life, by intentionally putting one's self in harm's way with the intent of being killed, cloaked in the excuse that it is for the cause of Christ, is selfish, self-serving, and sinful.

A messenger must exercise prudence in the context of opposition. Jesus warns his disciples to "Be on your guard" (v. 17). He likely means that they should not naïvely entrust their well-being to anyone. Friends can quickly become foes, authorities can become antagonists, and peaceful neighbors can turn violent. Another prudent response is to "flee to another [place]" (v. 23). There are times when getting out of harm's way is the most appropriate course of action.

In their enthusiasm to serve Jesus, messengers should never wantonly waste their lives by courting martyrdom. The destruction of one's own life, by intentionally putting one's self in harm's way with the intent of being killed, cloaked in the excuse that it is for the cause of Christ, is selfish, self-serving, and sinful. Those who would attempt such a course are out for self-glory and the making of a name for themselves. It is their hope that others would applaud them for their "sacrificial" action and thus bring to them a degree of admiration that they could not achieve otherwise. These overly zealous acts differ little from that of a fanatical suicide bomber from another religion.

Courage

Fear is a natural response to persecution, and Jesus was well aware of that. Three times in this passage he tells his disciples not to be afraid. He reminds them to look at the bigger picture. First, he reminds them that truth will ultimately prevail: "There is nothing concealed that will not be disclosed, or hidden that will not be made known" (v. 26). In the end, God will correct that which has brought harm and injustice to his messengers.

Secondly, he reminds them that no judgment which others may inflict upon a messenger can compare with the ultimate fate of those who do the inflicting: "Do not be afraid of those who kill the body but cannot kill the soul. Rather, be afraid of the One who can destroy both soul and body in hell" (v. 28). While it may be true that persecutors can kill a person's physical body, only God can condemn a person's soul to eternal death. That's even worse.

Thirdly, God's messengers, because of God's loving and watchful care for them, should not be afraid.

> *Are not two sparrows sold for a penny? Yet not one of them will fall to the ground apart from the will of your Father. And even the very hairs of your head are all numbered. So don't be afraid; you are worth more than many sparrows. (Matt 10:29–31).*

As already mentioned, God does not send messengers out carelessly. With these tender words, he proves it! He is not capricious in his watch and care over his loved ones, no matter where they are sent. A person's worth, especially a redeemed person's worth, is more valuable to him than the sum total of all other creatures. God is genuinely concerned when messengers pay a high price for serving him.

Discretion

Jesus colorfully draws from the animal world to bring to bear the necessity of his messengers to conduct themselves with discretion. He put it this way: I am sending you out like sheep among wolves. Therefore, be as shrewd as snakes and as innocent as doves (v. 16).

If members of the animal kingdom can show discretion in survival, how much more should God's servants? The servant of Christ should conduct himself in a manner worthy of Christ even in the midst of persecution. He should be like a sheep, a snake, and a dove all at the same time. It is instructive to take a look at these three comparisons.

Sheep, when attacked, do not have the ability to retaliate—they are hopelessly harmless. In the same way, Christ's messengers should exercise a demeanor of harmlessness even when under attack.

Then there is the snake, which has a reputation for its shrewdness and keenness. These two characteristics are recommended as human qualities,

105

involving insight into the nature of things and circumspection, common sense, and wisdom to do the right thing at the right time in the right manner.

Finally, Jesus mentions the dove, which symbolizes peace and innocence. This creature reminds us that neither wrongdoing nor questionable practices should mar the reputation of God's servant who is under fire. He is called upon to be discreet in his response, no matter how trying the situation, living uprightly in the midst of contemptuous circumstances.

Comfort in Persecution

Jesus has detailed the cost of serving as one of his messengers. He has made it clear that he would not send anyone out carelessly nor clueless about the dangers they would encounter. These truths are evident up to this point. Finally, he explains that neither would he send them out comfortless. Comforting clauses are found throughout his discourse. Jesus knew these words of reassurance were important in giving peace of heart and fortitude in mind to those who would face opposition.

There is comfort in knowing that it is Jesus who puts us on mission with him: "I am sending you out …" (v. 16). The double pronoun and choice of the word *send* can better read, "I myself am commissioning you." Granted, some may say that by their own free will they have chosen to serve, or volunteered themselves to Christ's cause, and maybe to an extent that is true. But there is great comfort in knowing that it is ultimately Jesus who sends messengers to do his bidding, especially into hostile environments.

There is comfort in knowing that if put in the position of having to defend one's ministry, that one should "not worry about what to say or how to say it. At that time you will be given what to say, for it will not be you speaking, but the Spirit of your Father speaking through you" (vv. 19–20). God will provide the words for a proper defense.

Finally, there is great comfort in knowing that in due course, "He who stands firm to the end will be saved" (v. 22). One way we prove that we have a redemptive relationship with God is evidenced by our unwavering loyalty to him to the very end. People don't allow themselves to be abused or to lay down their lives for Jesus unless they really and truly believe in him. They prove their genuine belief in him by their willingness to suffer for him.

Messengers of Jesus are both vulnerable and valuable.

Conclusion

It *is costly* to serve as a messenger of Jesus, and Jesus made this very clear in Matthew chapter 10. Some messengers pay a higher price than others. Some experience minimal opposition, whereas others are severely persecuted. Some serve with little discomfort, whereas others, like John Chau, pay with their very lives. All are expected to be aware of the fullness that is theirs in following Jesus, no matter what the cost. *The Manifesto for the Unreached* affirms, "We refuse to fear the darkness that entraps people when common sense says, 'protect yourself.' We will put on the armor of God and pray fervently for the sake of the unreached." (See the appendix.)

Messengers of Jesus are both vulnerable and valuable. David Sills, in his book *The Missionary Call*, helps keep Jesus' teaching on persecution and martyrdom in global perspective. He states,

> The dangers that exist are real, but only illustrate the fact that men and women need Christ. The suffering and dying of missionaries advance the Kingdom as nothing else could and the blood of the saints has ever been the seed and fuel of gospel advance."[76]

If we are to reach the remaining unreached, we must keep advancing, even in the face of hostility.

---

76 David Sills, *The Missionary Call* (Chicago: Moody, 2009).

REACHING A THIRD OF US

Those who engage in reaching the final unreached peoples will experience opposition and hostility. After all, one of the main reasons they are still unreached is because they are located in areas of the world that are the most hostile to the Christian message. Message-bearers must consider the cost to their well-being as they contemplate their part in taking the gospel to the remaining A Third of Us.

The discourse of Jesus found in Matthew 10 is the benchmark for understanding opposition, persecution, and martyrdom in the context of world evangelization. Through it, Jesus candidly covers the topic rather exhaustively. He speaks of the degrees of persecution, the sources of persecution, the attitude behind persecution, and the response we are to have to persecution. Jesus does not send out messengers who are clueless about the types and depths of opposition they will encounter as they engage the unreached.

CHAPTER 10

A Third of Us and You

"We can do it, if we will." —Samuel Mills

H ave you stopped to consider what role God would have you play in reaching frontier unreached peoples–those that make up A Third of Us? Maybe that is why you read this book—because you are seeking to determine that for yourself. Perhaps you have become so gripped with Jesus' command to reach the nations that you are exploring how you might contribute to that grand cause.

Obedience to the teachings of Jesus is seldom easy. Obeying his command to join the task of reaching the unreached can be especially daunting. To engage in it is not for the faint of heart nor for the weak in commitment. On one level, it takes a combination of willingness, determination, faith, and risk-taking for one to personally cross over into a foreign culture, and possibly live on foreign soil, in order to bring unreached peoples to the knowledge of Jesus. On another level, it may mean helping those who commit to such a path by rendering support through prayer, financial assistance, or just simple encouragement. Being obedient to Christ's call to reach the unreached will take you down one of these two paths.

> Obedience to the teachings of Jesus is seldom easy. Obeying his command to join the task of reaching the unreached can be especially daunting.

Whatever path we choose, those who willingly engage experience confidence and a settled mind in knowing they are doing what is dear to the heart of God. Can there be any cause more worthy than engaging in this mission of our Lord? Can there be any higher calling than to align our will with his? Can there be a better way to spend our lives, talents, and resources other than in this kind of commitment?

Giving up one's small ambitions and personal goals for eternal benefits should never be thought a waste. On the contrary, selfless sacrifice brings eternal gain (Phil 1:21). That is why martyred Jim Elliot, pioneer missionary to the unreached in Ecuador, could confidently write in his journal, "He is no fool who gives what he cannot keep to gain that which he cannot lose." There are no losers in the work of God, especially when we are bringing people to saving faith in Christ.

The responsibility of reaching the unreached was not lost on past generations. Samuel Mills, who was instrumental in propelling America into missions thanks to the famous "Haystack Prayer Meeting" in 1806, challenged a small band of fellow students with the now-famous words, "We can do it, if we will."

Today we have, at our disposal, all the resources necessary to finish the task. We have more—and better-educated—people; more financial resources; more material resources; more diverse, global Christians participating; and more-advanced technology available to us than any previous generation. However, the character quality most lacking, the character quality in which many today seem most deficient, is *the will to act*. Flipping Mill's statement: We can't do it, if we don't have *the will to do it*.

The Disparity
Mission Force

Although we have all the resources noted above at our disposal, a woeful disproportion of them are allocated to reaching the unreached. According to the newest edition of the *World Christian Encyclopedia*,[77] the total number of missionary workers globally is estimated at 425,000 (this includes all Christian traditions). Now on the surface, that seems like a lot of message-bearers crossing cultures with the good news. But the deeper question is this: What percentage of these workers are laboring among the unreached? And that's where it gets stickier.

Research tells us that there are 425,000 missionaries globally. With the proliferation of the "Majority World Church," coupled with its sending, missionaries today are being sent from most any nation in the world. A common phrase—or variations of it—being used today is "From everywhere to everywhere." Utilizing the World Population graphic found in chapter one, if we were to add missionary allocation on to it, it would show missionary distribution as follows:

77 Todd M. Johnson and Gina A. Zurlo, *World Christian Encyclopedia, 3rd edition* (Edinburgh: Edinburgh University Press, 2019).

Global Missionary Force

UNREACHED & UNSAVED No witnessing community within their people group or area. 3.2 billion / 41 percent	**No Access 3%**
UNDER-REACHED & UNSAVED Most have never had a clear presentation of the gospel, although it is nearby. 2.14 billion / 28 percent	**Some Access 20%**
REACHED BUT NOT SAVED Some knowledge of the gospel, nominal acceptance, "Traditional Christians" in name only. 1.56 billion / 20 percent — and — **REACHED & SAVED** True followers of Christ. 900 million / 11 percent	**Full Access 77%**

Based on this distribution, it should be noted that 77 percent of the missionary workforce is not focused on the unreached. That leaves 20 percent of the missionary workforce in places where "reached" and "evangelized" peoples are largely found, while the workforce focused on the really difficult, most unreached peoples—A Third of Us—is only 3 percent of all missionaries. Doesn't that sound like a disparity to you?

Mission Funding

Or take the matter of mission funding. The amount given to all of missions annually is about $45 billion. It is estimated that approximately $450 million of that is utilized in reaching the unreached—only 1 percent of all mission giving. Bearing in mind the vastness of the remaining task, that is a minuscule amount. As unbelievable as it may seem, someone has calculated that Americans spend more on Halloween customs—for their pets!—than the amount given to reach the unreached.[78]

---

78 http://www.thetravelingteam.org/stats.

What Others Have Said

If you feel hesitant about engaging in a meaningful way to reach A Third of Us, consider what others who have gone before us have said about reaching the unreached.[79]

"God has not asked us to reach every nation, tribe and tongue without intending it to be done." —Ralph Winter

"How do Christians discharge this trust committed to them? They let three-fourths of the world sleep the sleep of death, ignorant of the simple truth that a Savior died for them. Content if they can be useful in the little circle of their acquaintances, they quietly sit and see whole nations perish for the lack of knowledge." —Adoniram Judson

"God has called enough men and women to evangelize all the yet unreached tribes of the earth. Why do I believe that? Because everywhere I go, I constantly meet with men and women who say to me, 'When I was young I wanted to be a missionary, but I got married instead,' or, 'My parents dissuaded me,' or some such thing. No, it is not God who does not call. It is man who will not respond." —Isobel Kuhn

"The Great Commission is not an option to be considered; it is a command to be obeyed." —J. Hudson Taylor

"It is conceivable that God might have ordained to preach the gospel directly to man through dreams, visions, and revelations. But as a matter of fact he has not done this, but rather has committed the preaching to man, telling them to go and disciple all nations. The responsibility lies squarely on our shoulders." —J. Oswald Sanders

"Let us remind ourselves that the Great Commission was never qualified by clauses calling for advance only if funds were plentiful and no hardship or self-denial involved. On the contrary, we are told to expect tribulation and even persecution, but with it victory in Christ ... . It is ours to show, in the salvation of our Lord Jesus Christ, and in personal communion with him, a joy unspeakable and full of glory that cannot be affected by outside circumstances." —John Stam

"To know the will of God we need an open Bible and an open map." —William Carey

---

79 Quotes taken from, *Expect Great Things: Mission Quotes that Inform and Inspire*, by Marvin J. Newell (Pasadena: William Carey Library, 2013).

"If God has called you to China or any other place and you are sure in your own heart, let nothing deter you…. Remember it is God who has called you and it is the same as when He called Moses or Samuel." —Gladys Aylward

"If Jesus Christ be God and died for me, then no sacrifice can be too great for me to make for Him." —C. T. Studd

"None of us is beyond the task of missions… The question is not whether or not we will be working to spread the gospel around the world, but what role we will play in this." —Francis Chan

An Important Final Question

There is only one question left unanswered when it comes to reaching frontier unreached peoples: *What part are you willing to take?* Are you willing to engage it with passion and intention? Are you willing to be devoted for life? Can you go? If you can't go, can you commit to a supporting role of praying? Or giving? While it is true that God does not call all to go, he does call all to grow in a deeper understanding of his mission and then be a part of it in accordance to their capability. The support team is just as vital as those who serve on the front lines.

John Woodbridge asks, "What higher commission could a human being have than to be Christ's ambassador, His personal representative? Amazingly enough, that is the very mission to which each one of us as a Christian has been called: to be an ambassador for Christ. We are all on an awesome assignment in this life."[80]

Yes, to be an ambassador for Christ in reaching the unreached is what he asks of each of us. No believer should ever feel that he or she is exempt. Jesus will not excuse those who refuse to play even a small part. A widow's mite is just as valuable as a missionary on site.

A Dollar a Week for the Unreached

Speaking of a widow's mite, would you consider committing to be A Third of Us Advocate for the unreached? How can you do so?

---

80   John D. Woodbridge, *Ambassadors for Christ*, 10–11.

It's very easy. Set aside a dollar a week for the unreached. That's right, just one dollar a week! Then each year on Pentecost Sunday—the International Day for the Unreached—send your $52.00 to https://alliancefortheunreached. org/get-involved/. You'll be given the option to become an annual "Advocate" for the unreached. Join with many others to reach A Third of Us.

Promote Awareness
Here are two additional actions you can take to promote awareness of A Third of Us. Go to: https://athirdofus.com to check out these easy awareness actions:
1. Draw the A Third of Us symbol somewhere where it is visible, then look for opportunities to talk about it.

2. Download the Action Guide. In this free guide you'll learn more about the unreached and discover other specific actions you can take to bring the gospel to them.

A Final Word

I close by reminding all of us that over the past two millennia myriads of Christ-followers have ventured out in faith, joining Christ in his redemptive mission to mankind. They have had the boldness to do so based on the firm conviction that they personally were meant to be a part of the mission to the unreached. And so can you! His instructions are clear and precise. There is little danger in misinterpreting the nature of the task. Everything you need to know is found in the Great Commission commands of Christ. Place them at the center of your vision and passion, and you won't go wrong as you commit to reach A Third of Us. Commit with the confidence that you are doing what he has intended you, as a believer, to be doing all along.

If missions languish, it is because the whole life of godliness is feeble. The command to go everywhere and preach to everybody is not obeyed until the will is lost by self-surrender in the will of God. Living, praying, giving and going will always be found together.
—Arthur T. Pierson

APPENDIX

The Manifesto for the Unreached

Unengaged and Unreached People
We refuse to stand idly by as people enter eternity without Christ when we can share the good news that transforms them through any means possible. (Acts 5:40–42)

The Weak and Infirm
We refuse to watch people for whom Christ died suffer in pain and poverty when we can help restore them in His name. (1 John 3:17–18)

The Resistant
We refuse to fear the darkness that entraps people when common sense says, "protect yourself." We will put on the armor of God and pray fervently for the sake of the unreached. (Ephesians 6:10–20)

Partnership
We will release what God has given us to empower others to multiply God's kingdom through the gifts He has given them. (Romans 12:4–5)

Technology
We will leverage, to the best of our ability, God's gift of technology to reveal His eternal wisdom to those who have never heard the name of Jesus. (Habakkuk 2:2–3; 2 Timothy 4:2)

Resources
We will employ every resource, talent and ounce of energy God gives us to shine the light of His grace into the darkest recesses of the planet. (Matthew 25:14–30)

Declaration
We will shout from every peak, pinnacle and rooftop that the only hope for this dying world is a relationship with Jesus Christ. (Psalm 96:2–5; Acts 4:12)

Summary
As long as God provides His abundant grace, we will not stop or be deterred from this calling. We work relentlessly for the day when a gaze around the expanse of heaven reveals thousands worshiping at Jesus' feet because of the mission He gave us for this moment in eternity. (Revelation 5:9–10)

BIBLIOGRAPHY

Alford, Henry. *The Greek Testament*. Chicago: Moody, 1958.

Arias, Mortimer. *The Great Commission: Biblical Models for Evangelism*. Nashville: Abingdon Press, 1992.

Banks, William. *In Search of the Great Commission*. Chicago: Moody, 1991.

Barclay, William. *The Gospel of Matthew*. Vol. 1, Philadelphia: Westminster Press, 1975.

Barna, George. *Growing True Disciples*. Colorado Springs: Waterbook Press, 2001.

Barrett, David, Todd Johnson, and Peter Crossing. "Christian World Communions: Five Overviews of Global Christianity, AD 1800–2025." *International Bulletin of Missionary Research* 33, no. 1, 2009.

Bishop, Camille F. *We're in This Boat Together*. Colorado Springs: Authentic, 2008.

Blomberg, Craig L. *Jesus and the Gospels*. Nashville: Broadman & Holman Publishers, 1997.

Blue, Ron. *Evangelism and Missions*. Nashville: Word Publishing, 2001.

Bosch, David J. *Transforming Mission*. New York: Orbis Books, 1993.

Bridges, Jerry, and Bob Bevington. *The Bookends of the Christian Life*. Wheaton, IL: Crossway Books, 2009.

Bruce, Alexander Balmain. *The Expositor's Greek Testament*. Edited by W. Robertson Nicoll. Grand Rapids: Eerdmans, 1974.

Cate, Patrick O. *Through God's Eyes*. Pasadena, CA: William Carey Library, 2004.

Coleman, Robert E. *The Master Plan of Evangelism*, 30th anniversary edition. Grand Rapids: Fleming H. Revell, 1993.

Corduan, Winfried. *Neighboring Faiths*. Downers Grove, IL: InterVarsity Press, 1998.

Crockett, William V., and James G. Sigountos, eds. *Through No Fault of Their Own? The Fate of Those Who Have Never Heard*. Grand Rapids: Baker, 1991.

Dowsett, Rose. *The Great Commission*. Grand Rapids: Monarch Books, 2001.

Edwards, David, *with a response from John Stott*. *Evangelical Essentials: A Liberal-Evangelical Dialogue*. Downers Grove, IL: InterVarsity Press, 1988.

Effa, Allen. "The Greening of Mission." *International Bulletin of Missionary Research* 32, no. 4, October 2008.

Encarta' World English Dictionary ©1999 Microsoft Corporation. All rights reserved. Developed for Microsoft by Bloomsbury Publishing.

Engel, James F., and William A. Dyrness. *Changing the Mind of Missions.* Downers Grove, IL: InterVarsity Press, 2000.

Fletcher, Richard. *Barbarian Conversion: From Paganism to Christianity.* New York: Henry Holt, 1997.

Gallagher, Robert L., and Paul Hertig, eds. *Mission in Acts: Ancient Narratives in Contemporary Context.* New York: Orbis Books, 2004.

Gentry, Kenneth L. Jr. *The Greatness of the Great Commission.* Tyler, TX: Institute for Christian Economics, 1990.

George, Timothy. "Big-Picture Faith." *Christianity Today,* October 23, 2000.

Glover, Robert Hall. *The Bible Basis of Missions.* Los Angeles: Bible House of Los Angeles, 1946.

Harris, John. *The Great Commission or The Christian Church Constituted and Charged to Convey the Gospel to the World.* Boston: Gould, 1848.

Hendriksen, William. *The New Testament Commentary–Matthew.* Grand Rapids: Baker Book House, 1975.

Hesselbein, Frances. *Hesselbein on Leadership.* San Francisco: Jossey-Bass, 2002.

Hesselgrave, David. "Redefining Holism," *Evangelical Missions Quarterly* 35, no. 3 (July 1999): 278–84.

Howard, David M. *The Great Commission for Today.* Downers Grove, IL: InterVarsity Press, 1976.

Johnstone, Patrick. *The Church Is Bigger Than You Think.* Great Britain: Christian Focus Publications, 1998.

Kane, J. Herbert. *Christian Missions in Biblical Perspective.* Grand Rapids: Baker Book House, 1976.

———. *The Christian World Mission: Today and Tomorrow.* Grand Rapids: Baker Book House, 1981.

Klauber, Martin I., and Scott M. Maetsch. *The Great Commission: Evangelicals and the History of World Missions.* Nashville: B&H Academic, 2008.

Kostemberger, Andreas J., and Peter T. O'Brien. *Salvation to the Ends of the Earth.* Downers Grove, IL: InterVarsity Press, 2001.

Kouzes, James M., and Barry Z. Posner. *Leadership Challenge.* 3rd ed. San Francisco: Jossey-Bass, 2002.

Latourette, Kenneth Scott. *These Sought a Country.* New York: Harper and Brothers, 1950.

Little, Christopher. "What Makes Mission Christian." *International Journal of Frontier Missiology,* April-June 2008.

Mandryk, Jason. "State of the Gospel." Slide presentation, 2006.

Moreau, A. Scott, ed. *Evangelical Dictionary of World Missions.* Grand Rapids: Baker Books, 2000.

Neill, Stephen. *Creative Tension.* London: Edinburgh Press, 1959, 81.

Newbigin, Lesslie. *The Household of God.* SCM, 1953.

Newell, Marvin J. *A Martyr's Grace.* Chicago: Moody, 2006.

Nida, Eugene A., and William D. Reyburn. *Meaning Across Culture.* Maryknoll, NY: Orbis, 1981.

Olson, Gordon. *Beyond Calvinism and Arminianism.* Cedar Knolls, NJ: Global Gospel Publishers, 2002.

Pentecost, J. Dwight. *The Words and Works of Jesus Christ.* Grand Rapids: Zondervan, 1981.

Peters, George. *A Biblical Theology of Missions.* Chicago: Moody, 1972.

Pinnock, Clark. "Fire, Then Nothing." *Christianity Today* 44, no. 10, March 20, 1987.

Piper, John. *Let the Nations Be Glad!* Grand Rapids: Baker Academic, 2003.

Rainer, Thom S., and Chuck Lawless. *The Challenge of the Great Commission* (n.p. Pinnacle Publishing), 107–8.

Sanneh, Lamin. *Disciples of All Nations: Pillars of World Christianity.* New York: Oxford University Press, 2008.

Saurer, Erich. *The Dawn of World Redemption.* Translated by G. H. Lang. London: Paternoster, 1951.

Schirrmacher, Thomas. *International Journal for Religious Freedom.* Vol. 1, issue 1, 2008.

Schuit, Bill. "The Relay." In Currents Newsletter, by Leibenzell USA, Sept.–Oct. 2008.

Senior, Donald, and Carroll Stuhlmueller. *The Biblical Foundations for Mission.* Maryknoll, NY: Orbis Books, 1989.

Sills, David. *The Missionary Call.* Chicago: Moody, 2009.

Spurgeon, Charles Haddon. *The Gospel of Matthew.* Grand Rapids: Fleming H. Revell, 1987.

Stam, Cornelius. *Our Great Commission—What is it?* Stevens Point, WI: Worzella Publishing Company, 1974.

Stott, John R. W. *Christian Mission in the Modern World.* Downers Grove, IL: InterVarsity Press, 1975.

———. "The Great Commission." In *One Race, One Gospel, One Task*, Vol. 1. Edited by Carl F. H. Henry and W. S. Mooneyham. Minneapolis: World Wide Publications, 1967.

———. *The Message of Acts*. Downers Grove, IL: InterVarsity Press, 1990.

Taylor, Dr., and Mrs. Howard Taylor. *By Faith: Henry W. Frost and the China Inland Mission*. Singapore: OMF Books, 1988.

Taylor, LaTonya. "*The Church of O*." *Christianity Today*, April 1, 2002.

Taylor, William D., ed. *Global Missiology for the 21st Century*. Grand Rapids: Baker Academic, 2000.

Terry, John Mark, Ebbie Smith, and Justice Anderson. *Missiology*. Nashville: Broadman & Holman Publishers, 1998.

Van Rheenen, Gailyn. *Missions: Biblical Foundations & Contemporary Strategies*. Grand Rapids: Zondervan, 1996.

Vigeveno, H. S. *Thirteen Men Who Changed the World*. Glendale, CA: Regal Books, 1969.

Vine, W. E. *An Expository Dictionary of New Testament Words*. Westwood, NJ: Fleming H. Revell Company, 1966.

Walls, Andrew. *The Missionary Movement in Christian History*. Maryknoll, New York: Orbis Books, 2005.

Walls, Andrew, and Cathy Ross, eds. *Mission in the 21st Century*. London: Darton, Longman and Todd, 2008.

White, Karen. "Overcoming Resistance through Martyrdom." In *Reaching the Resistant*, edited by J. Dudley Woodbury. Evangelical Missiological Society Series, Number 6. Pasadena, CA: William Carey Library, 1998.

Winter, Ralph D., and Steven C. Hawthorne, eds. *Perspectives on the World Christian Movement, A Reader*. 3rd ed. Pasadena, CA: William Carey Library, 1999.

Wright, Christopher J. H. *The Mission of God*. Downers Grove, IL: IVP Academic, 2006.

Free PowerPoint Available

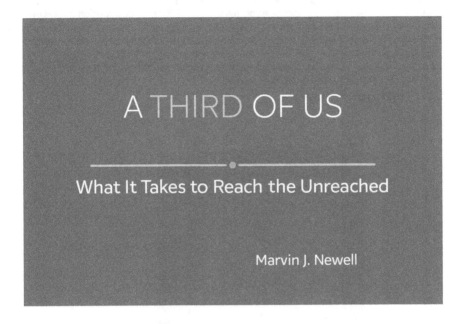

Do you want to teach from this book? The book makes for good mission instructional material, whether in a formal school setting, Sunday School, or small groups.

A FREE and easy to use PowerPoint aligned with the book's content is available at no cost. To download, go to the Alliance for the Unreached webpage. You will find it under the Resource tab:

https://alliancefortheunreached.org/resources

You have permission to add, subtract, or modify the PowerPoint to suit your teaching style and need.

Another compelling book by Marvin J. Newell

Expect Great Things
Mission Quotes That Inform and Inspire

Expect Great Things is the most comprehensive collection of mission quotes—contemporary and classical—ever compiled in one book. Here you will find over 700 of the best mission quotes ever uttered by Great Commission Christians—250 different authors from Adoniram Judson to John Piper, from J. Hudson Taylor to David Platt. Read them for personal encouragement! Paste them on your website, blog, or other social media. Tweet them to a friend. Include them in sermons, speeches, newsletters, and lesson plans. Pass them on to others to encourage them along their way to Great Commission familiarity and commitment.

$24.⁹⁹ | **368 Pages** | **Paperback**

Available at missionbooks.org

CPSIA information can be obtained
at www.ICGtesting.com
Printed in the USA
BVHW030301081122
651113BV00006B/13

9 781645 084037